A view of the Mansion's west side from the bowling green on a stormy summer afternoon.

A sunrise over the Potomac River viewed from the Mansion's piazza. OPPOSITE: *Washington planned his days carefully and kept a close watch on the time. He owned numerous timepieces, including this sundial, which sat atop a wooden post at the center of the Mansion circle and is now on view in the Museum.*

Plan Your Visit

FORD ORIENTATION CENTER

Start your Mount Vernon experience in the Ford Orientation Center, where you can watch the 25-minute action-adventure movie *We Fight to Be Free* and inspect a precisely crafted scale model of the Washingtons' famous Mansion. Maps in several languages and alternate formats, audio tours, and memberships are also available here. For more details, see pages 27–31.

For additional resources, including maps, tours, games, and quizzes, download the free app at MountVernon.org/app.

We recommend budgeting 45 minutes to visit the Ford Orientation Center.

MANSION

After the death of his older half-brother Lawrence in 1752, George Washington took up residence in the house that his father, Augustine Washington, built in 1735. Over the next five decades, Washington greatly expanded the structure into an impressive 21-room residence with architectural features that reflected his growing status as a Virginia gentleman. Vibrant wall colors, intricate moldings, delicate plasterwork, extensive faux finishes, and elegant furnishings bespeak the Washingtons' wealth and aesthetic preferences. The interior of the Mansion has been meticulously restored to its appearance in 1799. Walk through the first and second floors, where history interpreters are posted to provide relevant information. For more about the Mansion, see pages 33–87. Also, take a deeper look at the Mansion and surrounding estate—including facts and locations not included on the in-person tour—by going to MountVernon.org/virtualtour.

Timed tickets for Mansion-line entry are issued when you purchase admission online or at the Ford Orientation Center.

Depending on the number of visitors at a given time, Mansion tours last between 15 and 45 minutes.

MANSION OUTBUILDINGS

In designing his estate, Washington organized the outbuildings, lanes, and gardens in ways that reveal both his practical nature and personal taste. Many of the Mansion's essential operations—such as laundry, spinning, and meat curing—were performed in these small structures, located along the north and south lanes. Explore more than a dozen outbuildings, including a working blacksmith shop that features daily demonstrations. For more about the outbuildings, see pages 91–111.

We recommend budgeting 30 minutes to explore the Mansion outbuildings.

GARDENS AND GROUNDS

Blessed with a proverbial green thumb, George Washington was the driving force behind the design of four separate gardens covering more than six acres that surround his home. The gardens served many purposes, from testing new varieties of plants to producing vegetables and fruit to providing lavish floral displays. Enjoy each of these gardens as well as the quarter-mile-long forest trail that winds through the wooded landscape of Mount Vernon. For more details on the gardens, see pages 121–31. Heritage-breed livestock—including sheep, hogs, and cattle—inhabit areas around the estate just as they did in Washington's time. For more about Mount Vernon's menagerie of rare-breed animals, see page 118.

We recommend budgeting 30 minutes to explore the upper, lower, and botanical gardens. Allow 15 minutes to walk the forest trail, which includes some steep and uneven gravel paths.

TOMB

George Washington died in the Mansion's master bedchamber on December 14, 1799. His will directed that he be buried on his beloved estate. He also chose a site for a new brick tomb to replace the original burial vault, which was deteriorating. The Tomb was completed in 1831, and the remains of Washington, his wife, Martha, and other family members were moved there. For more details, see page 133.

Special wreath-laying ceremonies take place from April through October. Inquire about ceremony times at the Ford Orientation Center information desk.

We recommend budgeting 15 minutes to visit the Tomb.

SLAVE BURIAL GROUND AND MEMORIALS

Two memorials honoring the slaves who lived at Mount Vernon mark their burial ground. Located 50 yards from the Tomb, this was the cemetery for slaves and free blacks who worked on the estate during the 1700s and first half of the 1800s. Because the graves are not marked, the identities and numbers of those interred are unknown. Reflect on the historical significance and impact of slavery while viewing the memorials, which were dedicated in 1929 and 1983. For more details, see page 135.

We recommend budgeting 15 minutes to visit the slave memorials.

PIONEER FARM

Although we honor Washington as a military commander and president, he saw himself first and foremost as a farmer. Recognizing the inadequacies of 18th-century farming techniques, he sought new approaches to agriculture by experimenting with crop rotation, fertilizers, plowing practices, and more. The four-acre Pioneer Farm includes a scrupulously crafted replica of Washington's ingenious 16-sided treading barn and a re-created slave cabin. For more information, see pages 137–39.

The Pioneer Farm is open from April through October. Shuttle service is offered between the Donald W. Reynolds Museum and Education Center and the farm from April through October.

We recommend budgeting 45 minutes to explore the Pioneer Farm.

THE WHARF AND POTOMAC RIVER

Washington's fishery was among the most successful of his various business ventures. In one season alone, the operation pulled about 1.3 million herring from the Potomac River. A modern wharf is located adjacent to the Pioneer Farm.

Visitors can travel to Mount Vernon via boats departing from Washington, D.C., and Alexandria, Virginia. They can also enjoy a 45-minute round-trip sightseeing cruise, offered from April through October, for which tickets are available at the Ford Orientation Center and aboard the boat. Shuttle service is offered between the Donald W. Reynolds Museum and Education Center and the wharf from April through October. Learn more about the river—and how Washington used it—on the display located at the wharf. For more details, see page 141.

DONALD W. REYNOLDS MUSEUM AND EDUCATION CENTER

The Donald W. Reynolds Museum and Education Center offers a range of memorable experiences. The Education Center traces Washington's life story through state-of-the-art gallery displays, a multimedia theater presentation, History Channel videos, and remarkably realistic life-sized figures of Washington. Learn about his childhood hardships, his adventures on the American frontier, his heroic and ultimately victorious leadership of the Continental Army, and his precedent-setting role as the nation's first president. Accessible from the Education Center, the Hands-on-History Center offers engaging activities for children ages three to eight.

A comprehensive collection of more than 500 objects is displayed in the Museum's seven galleries. Gain insight into George and Martha Washington's tastes, style, and personalities by looking at their personal possessions. The F. M. Kirby Foundation Gallery offers temporary exhibitions, which generally change once a year. For more about the Museum and Education Center, see pages 145–59.

We recommend budgeting 45 to 60 minutes to visit the Education Center and 30 to 45 minutes to visit the Museum.

GEORGE WASHINGTON'S DISTILLERY & GRISTMILL

Washington had a large stone gristmill built in 1770 and 1771 to increase his production of flour and cornmeal and thus export high-quality products to the West Indies, England, and Europe. In 1797 his Scottish farm manager, James Anderson, encouraged him to build a distillery adjacent to the gristmill. The distillery produced nearly 11,000 gallons of rye whiskey and other distilled products in 1799, making it one of the largest and most successful such operations in America. Fully functioning reconstructions of both commercial buildings—located 2.7 miles from the estate's main entrance on Mount Vernon Memorial Highway/Route 235—are open to visitors from April through October. For more details, see pages 161–67.

Shuttle service between the Donald W. Reynolds Museum and Education Center and the Distillery & Gristmill is offered from April to October.

We recommend budgeting 60 minutes to visit the Distillery & Gristmill. Parking is available on site.

Accessibility

Mount Vernon welcomes guests with special needs. The Ford Orientation Center, Donald W. Reynolds Museum and Education Center, and Mount Vernon Inn Complex are accessible. Although the 18th-century pathways in the historic area can be uneven in places, there is an accessible path linking the Orientation Center with the Mansion and the Museum and Education Center. Other amenities and special tours are available upon request. For details, visit our website, MountVernon.org, or inquire at the Ford Orientation Center.

Special Events

Enjoy annual daytime programs such as George Washington's Birthday Celebration, An American Celebration at Mount Vernon on July 4, and Christmas at Mount Vernon. Or visit after dark for popular wine festivals and candlelight tours. For details, see our website, MountVernon.org.

Character Interpreters

Immerse yourself in George Washington's world by interacting with costumed interpreters who portray key figures from Mount Vernon and the first president's life. Character interpreters can be found in the historic area daily. Inquire at the Ford Orientation Center for times and locations.

Shopping

The Shops at Mount Vernon offer a range of gifts, reproductions, and old-time toys and games. Available at The General's Store in the Ford Orientation Center are guidebooks, rain gear, cameras, and other items to facilitate your tour. The Lady Washington Shop, in the greenhouse slave quarters adjacent to the upper garden, has assorted gifts, heirloom plants, and seeds. The largest of The Shops, located in the Mount Vernon Inn complex, features a comprehensive George Washington-themed bookstore, a year-round Christmas corner, fine and estate jewelry, Virginia foods and wines, and reproductions of Mount Vernon treasures. For young visitors, there is an array of toys, T-shirts, and other souvenirs. The Shops offer shipping for visitors who do not want to carry purchases home. All sales proceeds support Mount Vernon's operations and mission, which is to preserve the estate while educating the public about Washington's life and legacy. Visit The Shops online at MountVernon.org.

Dining

The Mount Vernon Inn Complex has two dining options. The Food Court Pavilion offers quick and delicious selections for breakfast, lunch, and snacks. Visitors can purchase fresh salads and wraps, grilled Paninis, burgers, personal-size pan pizzas, freshly baked cookies, and both soft-serve and hand-scooped ice cream.

The Mount Vernon Inn restaurant serves lunch daily, brunch on Saturday and Sunday, and elegant candlelit dinners Tuesday through Saturday. Savor regional cuisine in one of six intimate dining rooms—two with fireplaces. Reservations for dinner are recommended; go to OpenTable.com, or call 703-780-0011. For tour groups, weddings, holiday parties, and corporate events, call the Catering Office at 703-799-6865.

Edward Savage's group portrait shows President Washington, Martha Washington, two of her grandchildren—George Washington (Washy) and Eleanor (Nelly) Parke Custis—and one of the family's enslaved house servants. This is a rare color stipple engraving that the artist presented to Mrs. Washington in the summer of 1799. It is believed to have hung over the dining room mantel.

George Washington Chronology

1674

John Washington, George's great-grandfather, is granted the Mount Vernon home site.

1726

Augustine Washington, George's father, acquires the Mount Vernon property from his sister, Mildred.

1732

FEBRUARY 22

George Washington, first child of Augustine and Mary Ball Washington, born at the family home in Popes Creek, Westmoreland County, Virginia.

1743

APRIL 12

Augustine Washington dies at age 49.

1749

JULY 20

Appointed surveyor of Culpeper County, Virginia.

1751

SEPTEMBER

Sails to Barbados with half-brother Lawrence Washington; stays until January.

1752

JULY 26

Lawrence dies at Mount Vernon.

NOVEMBER 6

George Washington appointed major in Virginia militia.

1754

JULY 4

Surrenders to French after defeat at Fort Necessity.

DECEMBER 17

Leases Mount Vernon from Lawrence Washington's widow, Ann.

1755

MAY 10

Appointed volunteer aide to British General Edward Braddock.

JULY 9

Braddock killed and his army defeated in combat at the Monongahela River. Washington praised for his courage in battle.

AUGUST 14

Appointed colonel and commander of Virginia regiment.

1758

JULY 24

Elected to Virginia House of Burgesses (representatives) for Frederick County; reelected 1761.

1759

JANUARY 6

Marries Martha Dandridge Custis, a young widow. Settles at Mount Vernon with Martha and her two young children, John (Jacky) Parke Custis and Martha (Patsy) Parke Custis, and adopts them.

1761

MARCH 14

Lawrence's widow, Ann, dies. George Washington inherits Mount Vernon.

1765

JULY 16
Elected to Virginia House of Burgesses for Fairfax County; reelected 1768, 1769, 1771, and 1774.

1774

AUGUST 5
Delegate to First Continental Congress in Philadelphia.

1775

MAY–JUNE
Delegate to Second Continental Congress, which appoints him commander in chief of the Continental Army.

JULY 3
Takes command of army in Cambridge, Massachusetts.

1776

MARCH 17
Washington's troops drive the British out of Boston after an eight-month siege.

JULY 4
Declaration of Independence signed.

DECEMBER 26
Washington's troops surprise and defeat Hessians at Trenton, New Jersey.

1777

SEPTEMBER AND OCTOBER
Americans defeated in battles of Brandywine and Germantown.

1778

JUNE 28
British defeated at Battle of Monmouth.

1780

JULY 11
French fleet and 7,000 troops, under the Comte de Rochambeau, land in Newport, Rhode Island.

1781

OCTOBER 19
British forces under General Charles Cornwallis surrender at Yorktown.

NOVEMBER 5
Jacky Custis dies at age 26. The Washingtons adopt his two youngest children, Eleanor (Nelly) and George Washington (Washy) Parke Custis, and raise them.

1783

JUNE 19 Elected president-general of the Society of the Cincinnati.

DECEMBER 4 Bids farewell to his officers at Fraunces Tavern in New York.

DECEMBER 23 Resigns as commander in chief before Congress in Annapolis.

1785

OCTOBER 2–17
French sculptor Jean-Antoine Houdon visits Mount Vernon and creates a portrait bust of Washington.

1787

MAY 25–SEPTEMBER 17
Serves as president of the Constitutional Convention in Philadelphia.

A miniature portrait of General Washington from about 1800, after an original by James Sharples.

1788

JUNE 21

New Hampshire ratifies U.S. Constitution—the ninth and deciding vote for adopting the document.

1789

FEBRUARY 4

Unanimously elected first U.S. president by the Electoral College.

APRIL 30

Inaugurated at Federal Hall in New York.

AUGUST 25

Mary Ball Washington dies at about age 80.

1790

NOVEMBER 27

Arrives in Philadelphia, the nation's temporary capital.

1791

DECEMBER 15

Bill of Rights ratified.

1792

DECEMBER 5

Unanimously reelected to a second presidential term.

1793

APRIL 22

Issues proclamation of U.S. neutrality after France goes to war with Britain and four European countries.

SEPTEMBER 18

Lays cornerstone for U.S. Capitol in the new Federal City (later Washington, D.C.).

1794

OCTOBER

Whiskey Rebellion collapses after Washington arrives to lead nearly 13,000 militia troops in western Pennsylvania.

1795

AUGUST 18

Signs Jay's Treaty with Britain.

1796

SEPTEMBER 19

Farewell Address published in Philadelphia's *American Daily Advertiser*.

1797

MARCH 4

Retires to Mount Vernon after inauguration of his successor, former vice-president John Adams.

1799

DECEMBER 14

George Washington dies at Mount Vernon and is buried in the family vault there four days later.

1802

MAY 22

Martha Washington dies at Mount Vernon at age 70.

Robert Field's 1801 miniature portrait of Martha Washington.

Mount Vernon Chronology

1853
The Mount Vernon Ladies' Association (MVLA), the nation's first historic-preservation organization, is formed to rescue and restore George Washington's home.

1860
MVLA completes purchase of the Mansion and 200 estate acres for $200,000, begins restoration, and opens home to the public.

1861
General Winfield Scott issues order declaring Mount Vernon neutral ground during the Civil War.

1916
Mount Vernon's first electrical system designed and installed by Thomas Edison.

1923
Henry Ford gives Mount Vernon its first fire truck.

1932
Washington's gristmill reconstructed on its original site by the Commonwealth of Virginia; no milling operations take place.

1951
Greenhouse and adjoining slave quarters reconstructed on their original site.

1955
MVLA Vice Regent Frances Payne Bolton purchases 500 acres along the Potomac River's Maryland shore, directly opposite Mount Vernon, to prevent proposed construction of an oil-tank facility and sewage-treatment plant.

1979–82
Scientific paint analysis of Mansion undertaken. Interior repainted in original 1790s colors.

1996
Replica of Washington's 16-sided wheat-treading barn built.

2006
Ford Orientation Center and Donald W. Reynolds Museum and Education Center open.

Slave cabin replica built at Pioneer Farm.

2007
Washington's distillery reconstructed on its original site.

2009
Blacksmith shop reconstructed on its original site.

2013
Washington's "New Room" restored.

Fred W. Smith National Library for the Study of George Washington opens.

The Mansion's east-facing two-story piazza—the structure's most distinctive feature—has since the late 18th century been a popular place to catch cool river breezes on summer days as well as to view the Potomac River and the Maryland countryside beyond. OPPOSITE: *Washington used this surveyor's compass to lay out fields and to help settle boundary-line disputes.*

Exploring Mount Vernon

FORD ORIENTATION CENTER

The Ford Orientation Center is a perfect place to begin your Mount Vernon experience. This impressive and inviting structure, opened in 2006, was made possible by the generous support of Ford Motor Company, whose relationship with Mount Vernon dates back to 1923, when Henry Ford gave the estate its first fire engine.

The Washington Family, circa 1785

Produced by StudioEIS, in Brooklyn, New York, these life-sized bronze sculptures of George and Martha Washington with grandchildren Nelly and Washy welcome visitors to the Ford Orientation Center. Many make this their first stop, delighting to see how they "measure up" to the Father of Our Country.

We Fight to Be Free

Momentous events in George Washington's life unfold in this 25-minute movie packed with action and drama, plus a little romance. *We Fight to Be Free* introduces guests to the "indispensable man," whose talents, interests, and accomplishments were numerous and extraordinary. The film takes viewers back in time to defining moments of the French and Indian War; to the courtship of a young, widowed Martha Dandridge Custis and her future husband; and to the tense days in the Revolutionary War before Washington's troops famously crossed the Delaware River, on December 25, 1776. In the closing scene, General Washington finally returns home to Mount Vernon after resigning his command and eight long years of leading the Continental Army in the fight for America's freedom.

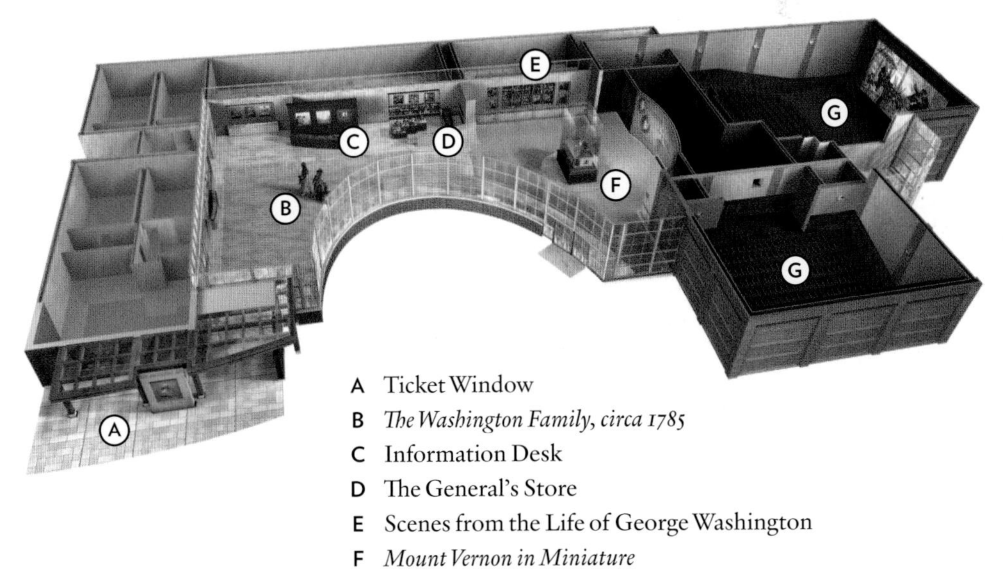

A Ticket Window
B *The Washington Family, circa 1785*
C Information Desk
D The General's Store
E Scenes from the Life of George Washington
F *Mount Vernon in Miniature*
G *We Fight to Be Free* Theaters

Screened continuously in the Ford Orientation Center's two theaters, We Fight to Be Free *vividly illustrates defining moments in Washington's military career, including this one during a battle in the French and Indian War.*

Scenes from the Life of George Washington

In 1997 Mount Vernon acquired this set of five stained-glass windows, which were created during the 1950s and 1960s in the studio of Karl J. Mueller. The colorful artwork includes depictions of Washington reading the Declaration of Independence, crossing the Delaware River, meeting with Alexander Hamilton, and taking the presidential oath of office, plus a playful rendering of young George chopping down a cherry tree—alluding to the myth originated by early Washington biographer Mason Locke Weems. The windows are now permanently installed in the Orientation Center's lower lobby.

Mount Vernon in Miniature

Completed in 1998, this unique handcrafted model of the Mansion and all its decorative contents was created by a group of more than 50 miniaturists, artisans, and Washington enthusiasts. Experts employed tools as varied as a mouse's whisker—to paint blue-and-white Chinese porcelain—to the "reduce" button on a photocopying machine to create small portraits.

Mount Vernon in Miniature weighs nearly 1,500 pounds and measures ten feet long, more than eight feet high, and about six feet wide. It duplicates the original building at a scale of one inch to one foot. A gift from the people of Washington State, it is displayed in a special glass case that reaches 16 feet to the ceiling.

MANSION

When George Washington began leasing Mount Vernon from his older half-brother Lawrence's widow in 1754, the house on the estate was smaller and less decorated, consisting of four rooms and a central passage on the first floor and three bedrooms on the second floor. During two major building expansions, Washington transformed the initial dwelling into the imposing Mansion visitors see today.

Although the residence was cobbled together over time, Washington's attention to detail and interest in design gave it an unusual harmony resulting from the compatibility of various architectural components.

He first expanded the house during 1758 and 1759, when he was starting to establish himself as a man of substance and style within the Virginia aristocracy. He increased the structure's height from one-and-a-half to two-and-a-half stories. Inside, he repainted, wallpapered, added wood paneling, reconfigured the staircase, and rearranged the second-floor rooms. For most of this time, he was hundreds of miles away, leading colonial soldiers against the French and their Indian allies. The young officer hired a skilled local craftsman to supervise the renovations, which his friend and neighbor George William Fairfax oversaw.

Washington began the second round of enlargements in 1775, just before the start of the Revolutionary War. At that time, his cousin Lund Washington served as farm manager and oversaw construction. During this phase, George Washington devised the features that make the Mansion truly impressive. He added a wing to either end and ordered construction of the piazza, colonnades, and two connected outbuildings—the servants' hall and the kitchen. The large dining room, the last interior space to be added, was finally completed several years after the end of the war.

Although Washington followed building fashions of the time, elements of the project express his own vision: the colonnades, which are open on both sides; the choice of a cupola for the top; and significantly, the two-story piazza that faces the Potomac River and remains Mount Vernon's most striking and oft-copied feature.

What to look for

CUPOLA: Washington added this architectural feature, generally found on public buildings, to the Mansion in part to help cool the house: hot air can be drawn out through its open windows. By providing a strong vertical axis, the cupola also helps disguise the asymmetry of the west facade, facing the bowling green.

WEATHERVANE: The weathervane atop the house decoratively incorporates a dove with an olive branch in its beak, symbolizing Washington's hopes for peace in the new nation. He commissioned the work from Philadelphia artisan Joseph Rakestraw while presiding at the Constitutional Convention during the spring and summer of 1787. The weathervane here is an exact replica of the original, which is preserved and on view in the Museum.

ABOVE: *Peter Waddell's 1998 painting* George Washington: Architect *depicts the Mansion during an early stage of its construction. The drawings at right show how the house grew over the years.*

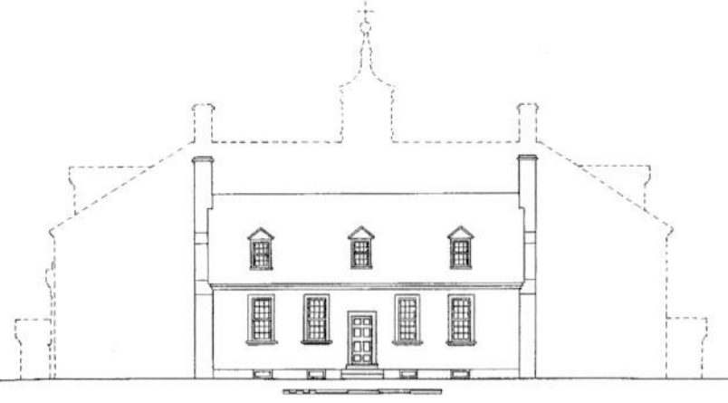

1757

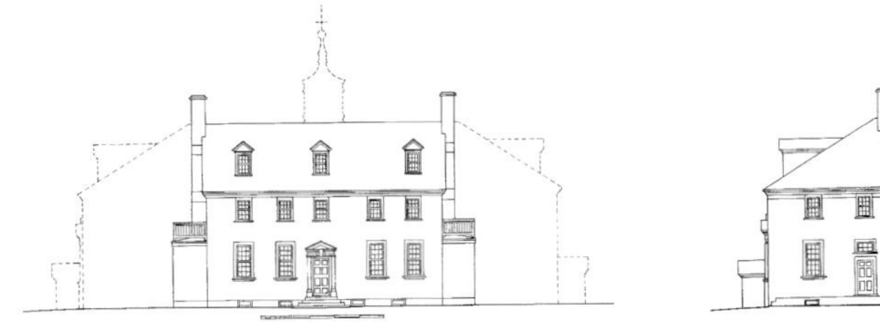

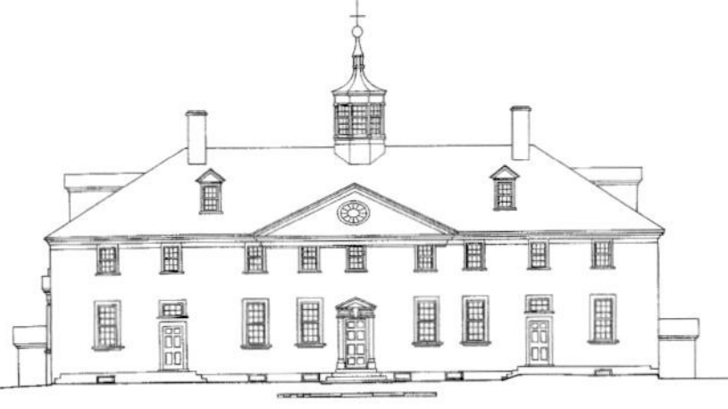

1792

Mansion Floor Plans

The Mansion's original cornerstone—on view in the Museum—bears the initials of George Washington's older half-brother Lawrence, who owned Mount Vernon from 1741 until his death in 1752. Lawrence substantially expanded the house he had inherited from their father, Augustine Washington.

THIRD FLOOR

- A Martha Washington's Garret Bedchamber, *pp. 82 and 83*
- B Garret Chambers
- C Lumber Rooms
- D Bull's-eye Room (china closet), *p. 83*
- E Cupola, *pp. 32 and 33*

SECOND FLOOR

- A Blue Bedchamber, *pp. 70 and 71*
- B Lafayette Bedchamber, *p. 66*
- C Hall Bedchamber, *p. 70*
- D Nelly Custis Bedchamber, *p. 69*
- E Yellow Bedchamber, *pp. 70 and 71*
- F The Washingtons' Bedchamber, *p. 73*

FIRST FLOOR

- A The "New Room," *p. 42*
- B West Parlor, *p. 56*
- C Little Parlor, *p. 55*
- D Central Passage, *p. 50*
- E Downstairs Bedchamber, *p. 60*
- F Dining Room, *p. 63*
- G Study, *p. 77*
- H Butler's Pantry, *p. 81*

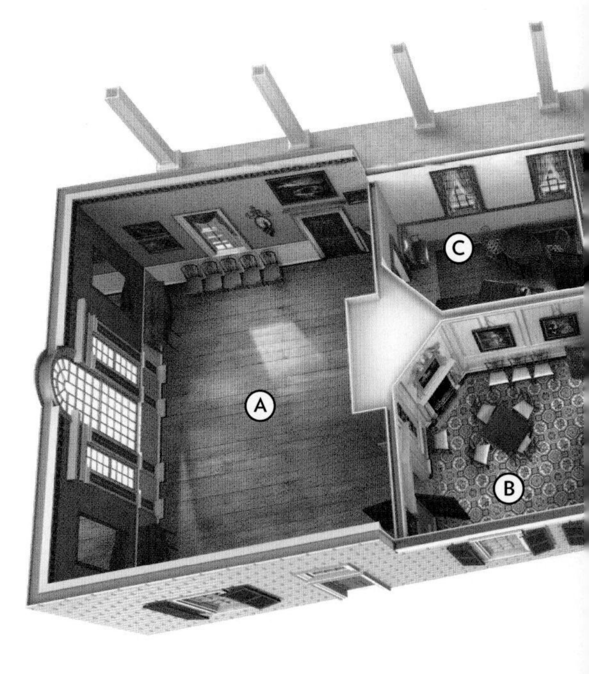

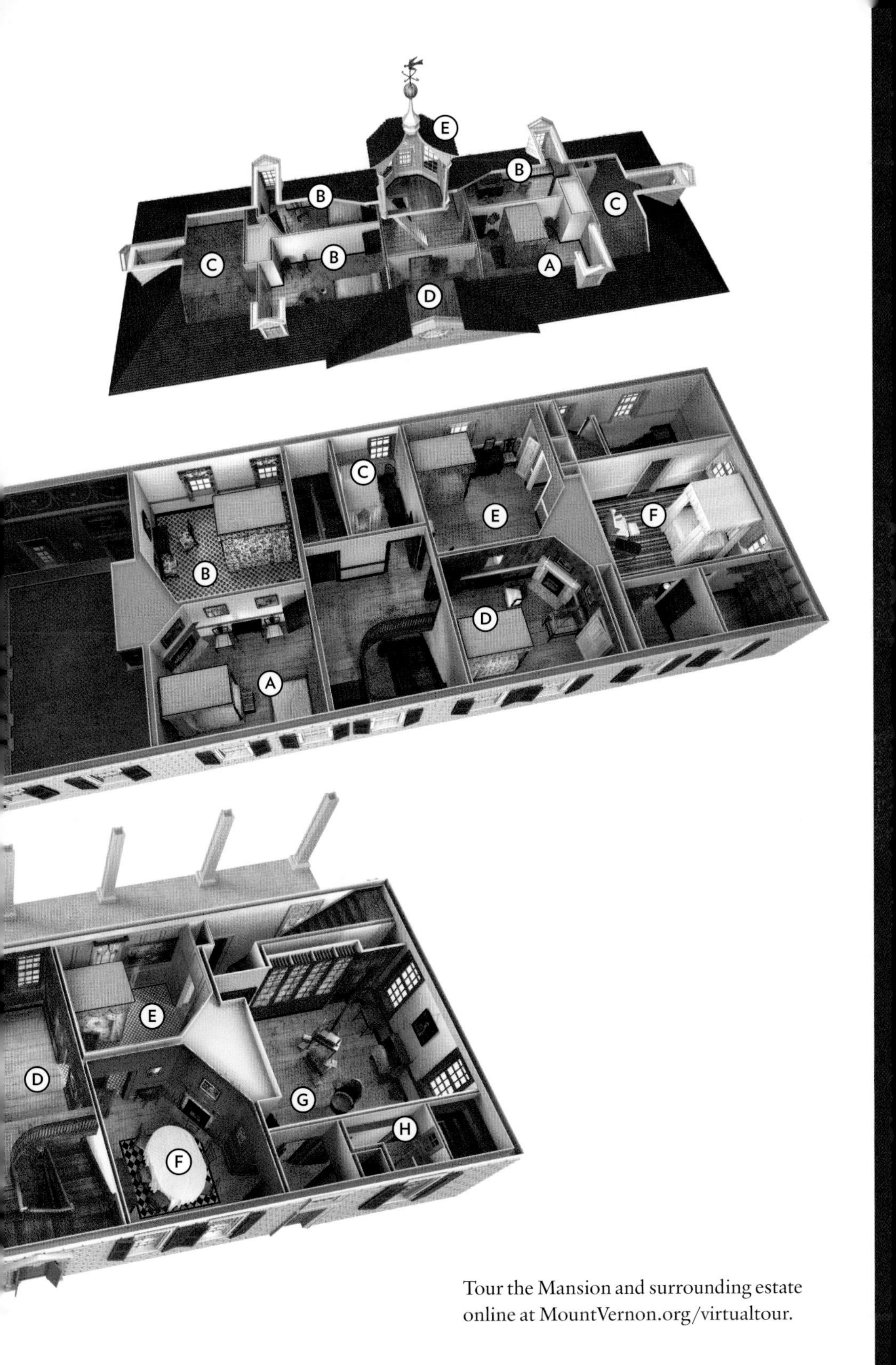

Tour the Mansion and surrounding estate online at MountVernon.org/virtualtour.

Servants' Hall

The first building visitors enter on their tour of the Mansion is the one-and-a-half story servants' hall.

Immediately obvious is the enormous fireplace, which looks somewhat out of place. Indeed, its construction was a mistake—an example of the challenges Washington faced trying to run his estate by writing letters from Revolutionary War encampments. His trusted farm manager and cousin, Lund Washington, at first misunderstood the purpose of the new building, thinking it was to house a laundry, as had the previous building on the site. By the time Washington's correction reached his cousin, an oversized fireplace for heating large kettles of water was already in place. Despite the presence of the unintended fireplace, the building became an accommodation for the servants of visitors and, sometimes, for strangers who arrived on Washington's doorstep to meet the new country's most famous man.

It was in the servants' hall in 1785 that renowned French sculptor Jean-Antoine Houdon created a life mask of Washington's face. The process was not a pleasant one, as the general had to remain perfectly still for at least 45 minutes with a mound of wet plaster molded to his face. The clay bust Houdon also created during this visit is prominently displayed in the Museum.

What to look for

RUSTICATED BOARDS: Washington enhanced the Mansion's modest frame exterior through a process called rustication, which entailed replacing the original plain wooden siding with boards beveled to look like cut-stone blocks. The wood was coated with paint and sand to create the appearance of stone, a more expensive building material.

The servants' hall (top left in this early morning view) is linked to the Mansion by the north colonnade. BOTTOM LEFT: *The south colonnade, connecting the Mansion to the kitchen (at the center of the view above), is supported by Tuscan columns and laced with trumpet honeysuckle.*

The "New Room"

Washington called this room—the biggest and grandest space in the house—his "New Room." With its two-story-high ceiling, detailed architectural ornament, and stylish furnishings, this room was intended to convey an emphasis on refined beauty and skilled craftsmanship, qualities he saw as communicating the new nation's values. Washington summed up his ambitious goals for the room in a letter written while he was off fighting the Revolutionary War: "I would have the whole executed in a masterly manner."

Opting for vivid paint and wallpaper through much of the house, he made choices that expressed the tastes of his era, when the use of bold colors was a sign of wealth. The stunning green of the wallpaper in this room was one of his favorites. The furnishings seen here include various original pieces—a number of them returned to Mount Vernon by descendants of the Washington and Custis families—and period pieces that are like those the Washingtons owned. Washington ordered the Federal-style sideboard (to the right of the large window, opposite) and several of the side chairs from a Philadelphia cabinetmaker near the end of his presidency.

Like the grand "salons" of fashionable 18th-century English country houses, this impressive room was meant to serve several functions. For example, its high ceiling and large, north-facing window made it an ideal picture gallery; the six large landscape paintings on display are the original canvases that Washington acquired and hung here.

The "New Room" was the scene of dinners for some of the many visitors who came to Mount Vernon in the post–Revolutionary War years. At 3 p.m., they were served the largest meal of the day, consisting of three courses. The first included various meats, vegetables, and side dishes; the second consisted of cakes, pies, ice creams, puddings, jellies, and cooked fruits; and the third included sweet wines, fresh fruit, and nuts. Washington was particularly fond of fish and Mrs. Washington of shellfish.

Washington also designed this room to be used for receptions and parties. With the table removed and chairs pushed back, there was plenty of space for dancing.

The design of this impressive Palladian window incorporates elements from Batty Langley's The City and Country Builder's and Workman's Treasury of Designs *(1740), an English pattern book that was popular with American gentlemen architects such as Washington.*

What to look for

MANTEL: After the Revolutionary War, Washington was famed throughout Europe, both for his military leadership and for relinquishing power to return to Mount Vernon at war's end. In 1785 he received this delicately carved marble mantel from Samuel Vaughan, an English admirer and friend, who sent it specifically for the "New Room." Created in the busy London workshop of sculptor Henry Cheere, the mantel features three idealized rural scenes: a farmyard well, a flock of sheep, and a boy hitching horses to a plow. These scenes beautifully expressed the two men's shared interest in agriculture and enthusiasm for the virtues of country life. Washington made this mantel—likely the only one of its kind in America at the time—the centerpiece of the room's decoration.

MOLDING: Visitors looking closely at the ceiling will see motifs Washington chose to illustrate his interests and his work. For example, the farming tools and grapevines symbolize the Earth's abundance and emphasize his role as an innovative and successful agriculturalist. The display of oak leaves and olive branches signify his hopes for America, representing strength and peace, respectively.

LANDSCAPES: Washington sought out artists who captured America's natural scenery. While president, he purchased six landscape paintings from two immigrant English artists, William Winstanley and George Beck. When he retired to Mount Vernon, in 1797, these six works were hung in this room. Two of Winstanley's canvases (including the one below) show idealized Hudson River views, while Beck's depict actual sites on the Potomac River, at Great Falls and Harpers Ferry.

Piazza

The two-story piazza is the Mansion's most distinctive architectural feature. Extending the full length of the east side of the house, it also has a practical function: catching the river breezes on hot and humid Virginia days. The Washingtons often treated the piazza as an outdoor room, serving afternoon tea here to visitors and family members seated in simple Windsor chairs.

"The situation of Mount Vernon is known to every one to be of surpassing beauty. . . . At the back of the house, overlooking the river, is a wide piazza, which was the general resort in the afternoon."

—Thomas Handasyd Perkins diary, summer 1796

What to look for

DEER PARK AND HANGING WOOD: From the piazza, visitors see the thickly wooded area that was a 16-acre deer park, a common feature on large estates of that time. Washington stocked his with tame deer from nearby and from England, for the delight of family and visitors. The trees between the Mansion and the river were carefully pruned to emphasize the view of the Potomac, creating a so-called hanging wood.

ABOVE LEFT: *John Gadsby Chapman painted this view of the east side of the Mansion in 1830s.* LEFT: *The Washington family enjoys an afternoon on the piazza, as depicted in 1796 by architect Benjamin Henry Latrobe.* RIGHT: *This silver urn, used for dispensing hot water during tea service (and visible in Latrobe's watercolor), is on view in the Museum.*

Central Passage

The central passage is the entryway into the Washingtons' home, the place where visitors who pulled up on the drive on the west side of the house were greeted. Entertaining also occurred in the central passage, particularly during hot Virginia summers when the family gathered here to enjoy breezes from the open doorways. The elegant space, which runs the width of the house, provides magnificent views of the Potomac and the Maryland shoreline to the east and of the pastoral bowling green, fields, and woods beyond to the west.

When George Washington first enlarged the house, in 1758 and 1759, he added the native black-walnut staircase to the central passage. Being prudent and practical, he moved the earlier staircase to provide access to the newly constructed third floor. The pine paneling on the first floor was also installed during the initial enlargement; later the paneling was grained, or painted, to imitate more expensive mahogany.

What to look for

BASTILLE KEY: A historic symbol of liberty, this key actually opened the main portal of the Bastille, the infamous political prison in Paris that was stormed at the outbreak of the French Revolution in 1789. The Marquis de Lafayette, who had served under Washington during the Revolutionary War, sent him the key in 1790, enclosing this note: "Give me leave, My dear General, to present you With a picture of the Bastille just as it looked a few days after I Had ordered its demolition, with the [main key] of that fortress of despotism—it is a tribute Which I owe as A Son to My Adoptive father, as an aid de Camp to My General, as a Missionary of liberty to its patriarch." The key still hangs where Washington installed it.

HANDRAIL: Millions of visitors have placed their hands where George Washington once rested his—on the handrail of this staircase.

Eighteenth-century visitors entered the Mansion through the west door, at the opposite end of the central passage from the Potomac-facing piazza. This door opened onto the circular driveway on the west side of the house. The Washingtons ordered the elegant ceiling lantern from London in 1760, along with 10 gallons of lamp "oyl."

Little Parlor

When George Washington returned home from the presidency, he decided to convert what had been a first-floor bedchamber into a music and family room, thus allowing more space for informal entertaining.

Music played an important role in the Mount Vernon household, as it did in other genteel Virginia homes of the period. Music masters traveled from plantation to plantation, instructing the young, and their presence often inspired lively social gatherings filled with music and dancing. Washington loved to dance, and he is reported on one occasion during the Revolutionary War to have done so for three hours.

Though by Washington's own account he could neither sing nor "raise a single note on any instrument," he helped ensure that his stepchildren and step-grandchildren were instructed in music. Early in his marriage, he ordered a spinet for Martha's daughter, Martha (Patsy) Parke Custis, and a violin and German flute for Martha's son, John (Jacky) Parke Custis.

What to look for

NEEDLEWORK CHAIR CUSHIONS: In 1765 the Washingtons ordered from London seven colors of wool yarn and one color of silk, "for working Cross stitch" on linen canvas, to make "one dozn Chair bottoms." Martha worked on this ambitious project over the course of three decades, finishing the needlework sometime after 1794—long after the seashell design had gone out of style. It is believed that the chair cushions made from the completed canvas work were used on Windsor chairs in the little parlor. The cushions on view are replicas of the originals, stitched in 2010 and 2011 by talented volunteer needleworkers.

MEZZOTINTS: While presiding over the Constitutional Convention in 1787, Washington agreed to sit for artist Charles Willson Peale, who wanted the general's image as part of a series of three men influential in the founding of the United States. These three small prints depicting Benjamin Franklin (left), George Washington (center), and the Marquis de Lafayette (right) were based on Peale's portrait studies.

West Parlor

Before the "New Room" was completed, Washington considered the west parlor to be "the best place in my House." This elegant room was a public space where visitors enjoyed the Washington family's company. Tea and coffee were customarily served here during the winter and on rainy days, and the household gathered here in the evenings to read, discuss the latest political news, and play games.

The architectural elements, including the mantel, two Palladian door frames, and paneled walls, make the west parlor one of the finest surviving examples of colonial Virginia architecture.

In 1787 changes were made to update the room, including the application of fashionable and expensive Prussian blue paint. The ceiling was also replaced and decorated in the neoclassical style. Reminders of the Washingtons are evident throughout the room, from the family portraits adorning the walls to the family coat of arms above the carved mantel and the crest on the decorative cast-iron fireback.

ABOVE: *John Wollaston painted a young Martha Dandridge Custis in 1757, shortly before the death of her first husband, Daniel Parke Custis. This piece is a 1981 copy by Adrian Lamb of the original work, which is in the collection of Washington and Lee University, Lexington, Virginia.*

LEFT: *This commanding likeness is an 1874 copy of the earliest-known portrait of Washington, painted in 1772 by Charles Willson Peale. Washington is impressively clad in the uniform of a Virginia Regiment colonel. A crimson sash crosses his chest, and a gilded gorget is suspended from his neck. Although Washington was 40 years old when he posed for the painting, it is meant to show him as he looked in his mid-twenties.*

What to look for

COAT OF ARMS: Carved into the pediment over the mantel, the Washington-family coat of arms includes a mythical griffin emerging from a coronet. Stars and bands complete the shield.

CREST: The family crest is cast into the iron fireback inside the fireplace. Under the crest, the cipher *GW* replaces the stars and bars in the shield of the coat of arms. Washington also used an adaptation of the family coat of arms in his bookplate (see lower right) with an accompanying Latin motto, *Exitus acta probat* (The end proves the deed).

SHARPLES PORTRAITS: These five portraits—of (top to bottom) Washington, Martha Washington, Georges Washington du Motier de Lafayette (son of the marquis), and Mrs. Washington's two youngest grandchildren, George Washington (Washy) Parke Custis and Eleanor (Nelly) Parke Custis—are pastel drawings by James Sharples. The inclusion of young Lafayette in this intimate grouping indicates the close ties between the two families.

OVERMANTEL LANDSCAPE: In 1757 George Washington ordered for the west parlor "a Neat Landskip 3 feet by 21½ Inches—1 Inch Margin for a Chimy." Designed to fit into the overmantel, this English scene was made by an unidentified artist in the style of the famous 17th-century French landscape painter Claude Lorraine.

A FAMILY OF HOUSE SLAVES

Visitors to Mount Vernon often were met at the door by Francis (Frank) Lee, who served as a waiter and butler. Though the majority of slaves at Mount Vernon worked hard and for long hours as plantation field hands, a select few were assigned to the house and gardens. Some of these favored house slaves developed relationships with the Washingtons that could be both close and complex.

During their early years at Mount Vernon, the Washingtons, like most other plantation owners, seem to have regarded slavery as integral and necessary to plantation life. After the Revolutionary War, George Washington expressed misgivings about slavery, and his last will and testament provided for the freeing of the slaves he owned. Still, both he and Martha expressed surprise and bitterness when, in the 1790s, two trusted house slaves—Hercules, a cook, and Oney Judge, a personal servant to Mrs. Washington—fled to freedom.

The Washingtons gave some of their enslaved workers responsible positions, including Frank Lee and several members of his family. Purchased by George Washington in 1768 along with his brother, Billy, Frank ultimately attained the position of butler. His wife, Lucy, was a cook at Mount Vernon. The couple had at least three children.

Billy Lee was Washington's personal servant for the eight years of the Revolutionary War. After sustaining injuries in a series of accidents during the 1780s, Billy could no longer carry out that role, so he took over the job of making shoes for other Mount Vernon slaves. Washington willed Billy Lee an annuity in gratitude for his loyalty, and he was freed when his master died.

Downstairs Bedchamber

This bedchamber accommodated some of the many visitors who stopped at Mount Vernon before, and especially after, George Washington's presidency. He once described the house as a "well resorted tavern" because "scarcely any strangers who are going from north to south, or from south to north do not spend a day or two at it." According to his diaries, overnight visitors were present in his home about two-thirds of the time. In December 1799, the household included six people: the Washingtons; Mrs. Washington's youngest grandchildren, Washy and Nelly Custis; Washington's nephew Lawrence Lewis, who had married Nelly in February of that year; and the Lewises' newborn daughter, Frances.

What to look for

VENETIAN BLIND: In 1787 Washington installed interior venetian blinds in all the Mansion's first-floor windows. The blinds were needed to regulate light and air because the exterior shutters were made of solid panels. By 1799, however, most of the downstairs shutters had been replaced with louvered ones, and all the venetian blinds had been removed except for this one, presumably left in place to ensure privacy for the room's occupants. In 2001 Mount Vernon restoration-staff members meticulously recreated the blind, based on period references and a few surviving examples.

PAINTING: The painting in the room depicts the Battle of Minden, in 1759, in which the Marquis de Lafayette's father was killed. A 1787 gift to Washington from his English friend Samuel Vaughan—who also gave him the marble mantel in the large dining room—it first hung in that room. Washington later moved it here to make way for a landscape painting over the Vaughan mantel.

Dining Room

One of the most striking spaces in the Mansion, the dining room is part of the original house, which was built in 1735. Over the years, the room underwent a series of renovations. While Washington was away with the Continental Army in 1775, it was updated under the supervision of his cousin Lund Washington. In 1785 striking verdigris-green paint was added. Washington believed the color to be "grateful to the Eye" and less likely than other colors to fade; an overcoat of glaze further intensified the color.

"The Stoco man is at worck upon the dineg Room. God knows when he will get done."

—Lund Washington to George Washington, October 22, 1775

What to look for

STUCCO WORK: In 1775 Washington decided to install an elaborately decorated plaster ceiling and add plaster ornaments above the fireplace. He hired an expert plasterer, identified simply as the "stucco man," who spent five months completing the hand-tooled ceiling. A renovation in 2001 uncovered some of his original pencil drawings on the ceiling, laying out the design.

LIQUOR CHEST: In 1761 Washington complained to his London purchasing agent about the high price he was charged for this 16-bottle mahogany chest, contending that he could have had it made locally at a much lower cost.

MANTEL: The ornate rococo design was chosen from *The British Architect*, Abraham Swan's popular design book of 1758.

BLUE-AND-WHITE PORCELAIN: Washington ordered blue-and-white Chinese export porcelain at least nine times over a span of 34 years. Chinese porcelain was fashionable in England and America, and the Washingtons owned several different patterns. When Martha Washington died, in 1802, she bequeathed the blue-and-white porcelain—the china "in common use"—to her granddaughter Nelly.

Lafayette Bedchamber

This room is often called the Lafayette bedchamber because it is believed that the marquis stayed here while visiting the Washingtons. Lafayette was a young French nobleman who volunteered his services in America's fight for freedom. Like his beloved Washington, he served without pay as a general in the Continental Army, and the two maintained a strong bond.

What to look for

PORTRAIT OF LAFAYETTE: A period likeness of Lafayette is on display in this room. In a 1784 letter to the marquis, George Washington wrote, "It is unnecessary, I [persuade] myself to repeat to you my [dear] Marqs. the sincerity of my regards & friendship—nor have I words which could express my affection for you, were I to attempt it."

Nelly Custis Bedchamber

This room was used by Martha Washington's granddaughter Eleanor (Nelly) Parke Custis, who lived at Mount Vernon from early childhood. The room was part of the 1758–59 enlargement of the house, and much of the plaster and woodwork are original. As with other rooms in the Mansion, a more fashionable paint color was added to the walls in the 1780s, and there is evidence that the room once had blue wallpaper.

Nelly married George Washington's nephew Lawrence Lewis at Mount Vernon on February 22, 1799—the president's last birthday. The couple lived at Mount Vernon until construction of their home, Woodlawn Plantation, three miles away, was completed. Their first child, Frances, was born in this room in December 1799, only days before Washington's death. Nelly remained confined to her bed and was unable to attend her step-grandfather's funeral.

What to look for

CRIB: The mahogany crib was a gift from Martha Washington to her granddaughter. Its first occupant was Frances Parke Lewis, Nelly's firstborn. The tester and tops of posts were later additions. One of the sides folds down, for easier access—at that time a recent innovation in crib design.

English artist James Sharples's pastel portrait of Nelly Custis hangs in the Mansion's west parlor.

Other Bedchambers

The Washingtons welcomed hundreds of visitors to Mount Vernon each year, and Martha Washington was often praised for her well-run household. Many of these visitors stayed overnight, or for several days, and the servants were kept busy preparing rooms to accommodate them. Mrs. Washington kept low-post beds in storage that could be set up to meet the needs of the overflow of travelers.

Elkanah Watson, who visited in 1785, described the kind of personal attention a guest might receive. Although he was a stranger to George Washington, Watson arrived with letters of introduction from several of the general's close friends. The Washingtons served him dinner and engaged him in affable conversation, after which he went to bed "oppressed by a severe cold." Then, as he recounted in his journal: "As usual after retiring, my coughing increased. When some time had elapsed, the door of my room was gently opened, and on drawing my bed-curtains, to my utter astonishment, I beheld Washington himself, standing at my bed-side, with a bowl of hot tea in his hand."

ABOVE: *This silver-plated candlestick Washington owned is fitted with a removable, slightly cupped collar to catch dripping wax and make cleaning easier.*
RIGHT: *This porcelain bowl and saucer are from a Chinese-export tea set purchased by Washington.*

The Washingtons' Bedchamber

Located directly above the study in the private south wing is George and Martha Washington's spacious bedroom. Designed according to Mrs. Washington's suggestion that it be simple and functional, the room was also her sanctuary, where she planned her schedule and wrote letters to friends and family members. According to her grandson, she also spent an hour each day reading the Bible and praying.

Washington died of a severe throat infection in this room on December 14, 1799. Upon his death, Martha closed the room and, for the remaining several years of her life, spent much of her time in a bedchamber on the third floor.

What to look for

BED: Purchased in the early 1790s, this bed was described by Mrs. Washington as "the new bedstead which I caused to be made in Philadelphia." Its design is in keeping with the Washingtons' preference for elegant simplicity. At just over six feet six inches long, it was large enough to accommodate George Washington, who stood about six feet two inches tall.

PINE PORTRAITS: In 1785, at the request of friends, Washington agreed to sit for a portrait by Robert Edge Pine. While the artist was at Mount Vernon, Martha Washington apparently commissioned him to paint portraits of her four grandchildren, which were hung in the master bedroom.

Robert Edge Pine painted these portraits of Martha (Patty) Parke Custis (left) and Eleanor (Nelly) Parke Custis (right), two of Martha Washington's granddaughters.

MANTEL CLOCK: The clock is one of many items Washington brought back to Mount Vernon after his presidency ended. It is most likely the "Time Piece" valued at $100 that is listed in the 1799 inventory of the Washingtons' bedroom, making it one of the most expensive items they owned.

FRENCH WRITING DESK: Crafted of mahogany with a marble top and brass fittings, this desk, purchased in 1790, was used by Mrs. Washington in the presidential households in New York and Philadelphia and later at Mount Vernon. It is said that after her husband's death, she destroyed their personal correspondence. Only three letters are known to survive, two of which were inadvertently concealed behind a drawer in this desk.

Beauty and Prudence, *one of eight circular-framed engravings decorating the Washingtons' bedchamber.*

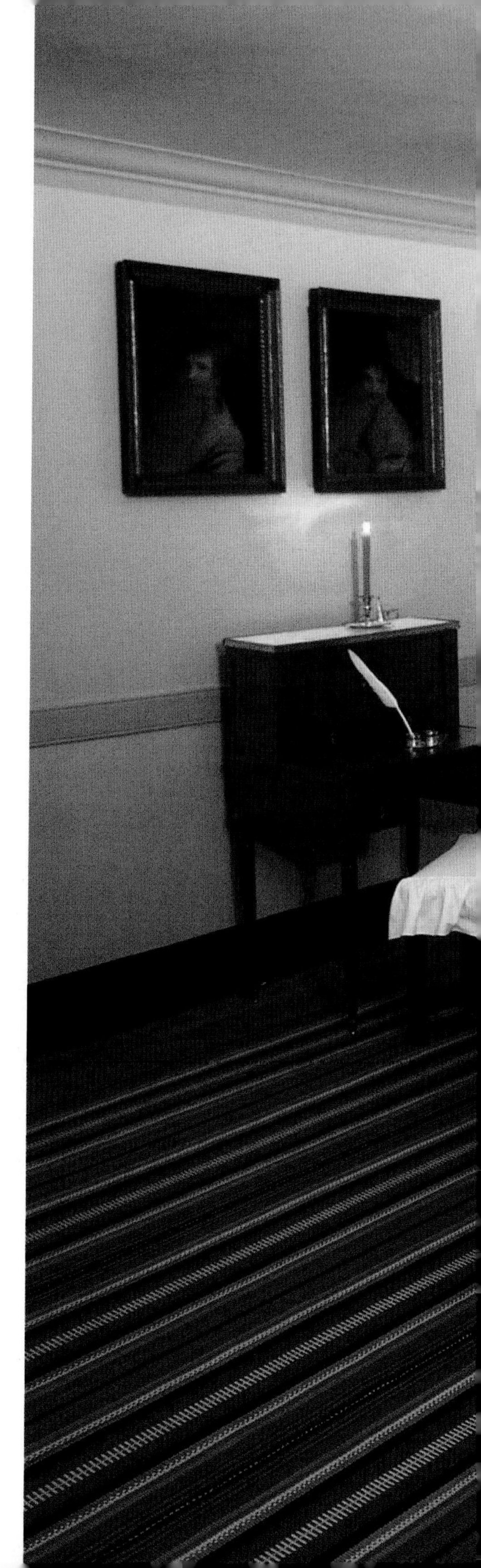

Study

After George Washington's return to Mount Vernon in 1783 at the end of the Revolutionary War, the study became the place where he could retreat from ever-present family and visitors and tend to business. Reportedly, no one was allowed in this room without his invitation. From here, he directed the management of his estate, receiving reports from overseers, making daily diary entries, and posting his accounts.

The study was also where Washington bathed, dressed, and kept his clothes. Each morning, he rose between 4 and 5 a.m. and went to the study, using the private staircase that led down from the bedchamber. According to the recollections of his step-grandson George Washington (Washy) Parke Custis, he lit his own fire and dressed himself. Washington used the quiet time to write letters or review reports until breakfast at 7 a.m., after which he usually rode out to his farms. In the evening, unless he had a social obligation or lingered talking to visitors after dinner, he returned here to read or confer with his secretary until around 9 p.m., when he went to bed.

What to look for

FAN CHAIR: While presiding over the Constitutional Convention in Philadelphia in 1787, Washington ordered a fan chair for use at Mount Vernon. Fond of contraptions and new inventions, he saw the chair demonstrated during his stay in that city. The apparatus consisted of a pasteboard fan connected to wooden treadles and attached to a Windsor chair; sitters moved the fan back and forth by pumping the pedals with their feet. This period example—one of just two known to exist—is similar to the chair Washington owned.

LAWRENCE WASHINGTON PORTRAIT: After Washington's father died, his half-brother Lawrence assumed the role of mentor to his younger sibling. Through him, Washington was introduced to some of Virginia's leading families, and was able to learn and practice the social graces as well as further his career as a surveyor.

"I conceive a knowledge of books is the basis upon which other knowledge is to be built."

—George Washington to
Jonathan Boucher, July 9, 1771

SECRETARY: In 1797 Washington sold the desk he used as president and bought a secretary (see opposite), which was made in Philadelphia by John Aitken. Stored on its bookshelves were a few of the more than 1,200 volumes in his personal library, which included works on history, politics, law, agriculture, military strategy, literature, and geography.

PRESIDENTIAL CHAIR: This was Washington's office chair throughout his presidency, in New York and later in Philadelphia. When he retired to Mount Vernon in 1797, he brought it home and placed it in his study. The chair features an unusual swivel mechanism that allows the seat to rotate on rollers.

TOP: *Washington's bound copy of the U.S. Constitution.* BOTTOM: *The title page of his copy of a four-volume edition of Lord Chesterfield's* Letters to His Son *(1774), famed for their guidelines on gentlemanly behavior, bears the first president's distinctive signature.*

Butler's Pantry

Everyday Chinese porcelain dishes were stored in this small space. A few surviving pieces are on display for closer inspection in the Museum. Finer china was stored in a closet on the third floor.

Evidence of the wiring for the house bell system can still be seen across the ceilings of the pantry and the yellow bedchamber. The bells summoned servants or slaves to the dining rooms, the piazza, and one of the bedrooms.

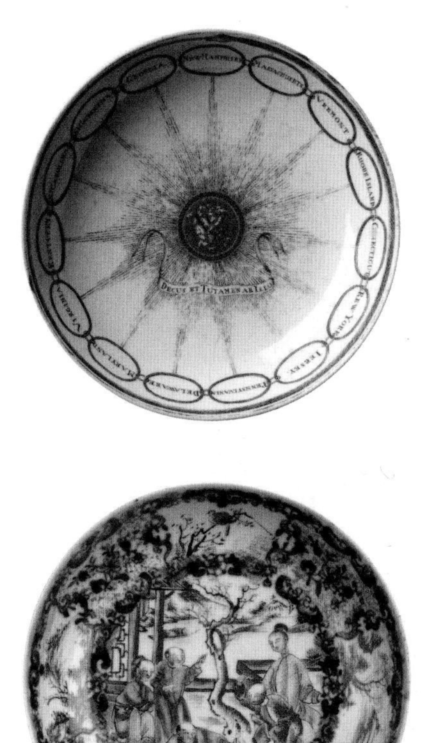

The Washingtons owned dishes in various patterns, including (clockwise from bottom left): monogrammed French porcelain; a handsome Chinese service bearing the insignia of the Society of the Cincinnati; a porcelain service, given by a Dutch merchant in 1796, that featured the 15 U.S. states as a chain encircling Martha Washington's monogram; and a colorful Chinese porcelain tea service, purchased in 1757.

Third Floor

The Mansion's third floor includes a number of rooms that were used for storage and living space. The area also provides access to the cupola. After her husband's death, Martha Washington retreated to a small bedchamber here. From this room and the adjoining area, she continued to manage the household and greet visitors. She died in this bedchamber on May 22, 1802.

"Tis well. All is now over. I have no more trials to pass through. I shall soon follow him."

—Martha Washington on the death of her husband, December 14, 1799

The Mansion's decorative bull's-eye window lights the third-floor china closet.

Kitchen

Mount Vernon's kitchen bustled with activity seven days a week. A staff comprised of a hired housekeeper and several enslaved workers—Frank the butler, cooks Nathan and Lucy, and a scullion or two—worked here under Martha Washington's supervision. Although it's not clear whether she did any actual cooking, she did plan meals and made sure the table was laid with well-prepared meats and fresh vegetables.

Days in the kitchen started early, so that breakfast could be on the table at 7 a.m. According to one visitor, it was "in the usual Virginia style," consisting of tea, coffee, and boiled and cold meats. According to his step-granddaughter Nelly Custis, Washington usually ate three small cornmeal hoecakes, "swimming in butter and honey," and drank three cups of tea without cream.

Dinner, the main meal of the day, usually was served at 3 p.m. Tea was served about 7 p.m., and supper—a light meal—was not served at all, according to one visitor, but according to another it was offered at 9 p.m. A guest at one of Mount Vernon's impressive midday meals wrote: "The dinner was very good, a small roasted pigg, boiled leg of lamb, roasted fowles, beef, peas, lettice, cucumbers, artichokes, etc., puddings, tarts, etc. etc. We were desired to call for what drinks we chose."

Putting the kitchen in a separate building, a practice common on Southern plantations, kept the noise, heat, and potential threat of fire away from the house.

What to look for

SCULLERY: The scullery provided additional space for food preparation and dishwashing.

UPSTAIRS: The stairway leads to two rooms: one was used for storing kitchen utensils, and the other was living space for the cooks or hired housekeeper. At the time of George Washington's death, the housekeeper was Mrs. Eleanor Forbes, who had filled the same role for the governor of Virginia.

UTENSILS: The crane in the kitchen fireplace is believed to be an original. The utensils displayed are period examples of items listed in inventories of the Mount Vernon kitchen.

LARDER: The larder was cooler than the rest of the kitchen because of its sunken floor. With the door closed to shut out heat from the fireplace, perishables could keep here for a day or two.

ABOVE: *Excavated in an archaeological dig near the kitchen, this pipkin may be one of several that Washington ordered from England in 1761. Pipkins are small earthenware pots and pans that, due to everyday use, rarely last long.*
LEFT: *The threat of fire was constant in 18th-century kitchens. Washington bought six leather fire buckets in 1797, one of which is on view in the Museum.*

Washington situated the Mansion's outbuildings where they would not intrude on views of either the bowling green or the Potomac.

36
GEO. WASHINGTON
VIRGINIA

SOUTH LANE OUTBUILDINGS

Storehouse, Clerk's Quarters, and Paint Cellar

George Washington and his farm managers kept a watchful eye on the storehouse, which was within sight of the Mansion. This building provided storage under lock and key for hundreds of items, such as tools and nails used by carpenters, leather and thread for the cobbler, powder and shot for the huntsmen, and blankets and clothes used by the slaves. Items were inventoried as they were purchased and then carefully issued as needed.

The clerk's quarters, in the same building, provided a residence and office for Washington's secretary. After the presidential years, Albin Rawlins filled this position, helping Washington with his correspondence and serving as a business agent for enterprises such as the gristmill. Rawlins's quarters were near the Mansion study, so his employer could quickly summon him.

The cellar of this building was used to store the expensive pigments that were painstakingly ground by hand and mixed with linseed oil to make house paint. Maintaining the painted surfaces of the Mansion and outbuildings was a continual, labor-intensive process.

OPPOSITE: *Tools and dry goods in the storehouse.* BELOW: *Accommodations in the clerk's quarters were spartan.*

Smokehouse

Vast quantities of pork—mainly bacon and ham—were smoked to feed the family and Mount Vernon's guests. Fish, fowl, and the meat of larger animals were eaten fresh as well as cured in order to last longer.

After enslaved workers salted or pickled the meat, they hung it on the rails inside the smokehouse above a smoldering fire that burned in the pit at the center of the building. For long-term storage after smoking, the meats remained hanging or were packed in barrels filled with ashes. During the curing process, meat was locked in the smokehouse to prevent theft. This precaution was not always successful, however. In May 1795, while President Washington was living in Philadelphia, his farm manager William Pearce wrote to inform him that "some person ripped a plank off the Back part of the smoke House and Took out several pieces of Bacon. . . . I have not been able to find out yet who It is."

According to Washington, Virginia ladies took special pride in the quality of the ham and bacon produced on their plantations. He and his wife even sent these meats as gifts to friends in far-off Europe. In 1786 the general wrote the Marquis de Lafayette that Mrs. Washington "had packed & sent . . . a barrel of Virginia Hams. I do not know that they are better, or so good as you make in France but as they are of our own manufacture . . . and we recollect that it is a dish of which you are fond."

ABOVE: *This silver-handled knife and fork were part of a large assortment of tableware that Washington ordered from England in 1757.* OPPOSITE: *The smokehouse interior (top) and a ham served in the Mansion's large dining room (bottom).*

Wash House and Laundry Yard

Washing laundry was a hot and difficult job. Enslaved women, including two named Vina and Dolsey, worked as washerwomen here. To do a load of laundry, they carried 25 to 30 buckets of water from a nearby well and boiled it in a hot-water stove. They plunged it into the hot water and hand-scrubbed the fabrics with a soap made of lye and animal fat. White fabrics were sometimes draped over bushes in the yard to dry because the combination of sunlight and the chlorophyll in the leaves worked as a natural bleach. Other items were hung on clotheslines. In wet weather, laundry was placed on wooden drying racks indoors. The washerwomen used irons heated in the fire and/or a large wooden mangle to press the laundry.

The constant stream of guests at Mount Vernon kept the washerwomen quite busy. One guest noted that the slaves "took care of me, of my linen, of my clothes," treating him "not as a stranger but as a member of the family." Given the often-confusing mix of family members and visitors, clothing and linens were frequently marked with their owners' initials in order to avoid mix-ups.

ABOVE: *Detail of a damask napkin bearing the Washingtons' laundry mark.* LEFT: *The wash house interior (top) and the dung repository (bottom).*

"When I speak of a knowing farmer, I mean . . . above all, Midas like, one who can convert everything he touches into manure, as the first transmutation towards Gold."

—George Washington to George William Fairfax, June 30, 1785

Dung Repository

The "Repository for Dung," as it was known when completed, was designed to compost animal droppings and other organic waste for use as fertilizer in the nearby gardens and orchards. The building illustrates Washington's dedication to finding ways to improve soil fertility and to making Mount Vernon a model of progressive farming.

The original 31-by-12-foot open-walled structure was erected in 1787. It was reconstructed in 2001, based on Washington's notes, historical documents discussing fertilizer production, and two years of archaeological excavation. Archaeologists revealed remnants of the brick foundation walls along the virtually intact cobblestone floor; these were incorporated into the reconstructed building. Washington's dung repository is thought to be the first structure in the nation specifically designed for composting.

Coach House and Stable

The area around the stable and coach house was always a hub of activity at Mount Vernon. George Washington was an excellent horseman who paid close attention to the care of his animals. Martha Washington, who encouraged women to ride for exercise, was an avid equestrian in her younger years.

Under the direction of Peter Hardiman, an enslaved worker whose talent with horses and mules greatly impressed Washington, other slaves fed and groomed the animals, cleaned harnesses and saddles, and collected manure for use as fertilizer. Their work increased rapidly with the delivery of mares sent to the plantation for breeding and also when the horses of visitors needed tending.

The stable dates back to Washington's lifetime, but the coach house was reconstructed on the original site in 1894.

What to look for

COACH: Travel by small coach was difficult during the 18th century. Poorly maintained roads meant that even short journeys could be hazardous and that vehicles wore out quickly. Enslaved workers such as Joe, a driver, and Jack, a wagoner, took care of Mount Vernon's vehicles. These included a small coach similar to the one shown at right, which, like Washington's, was crafted by well-known Philadelphia carriage makers David and Francis Clark.

RIDING CHAIR: As a young man, Washington acquired a riding chair similar to the 18th-century example displayed in the coach house alongside a modern reproduction (pictured below). Popular in America and England, riding chairs could travel country lanes and back roads more easily than bulkier four-wheeled chariots and coaches. They were also relatively inexpensive compared to other wheeled vehicles. Members of all social classes used riding chairs to traverse the rough Virginia terrain.

Though outbuildings were utilitarian, George Washington made sure they added to Mount Vernon's charm by covering them with white weatherboards and adorning them with red-painted wood shingles.

NORTH LANE OUTBUILDINGS

Gardener's House

This building (interior and exterior shown at left) first served briefly as a hospital for slaves, then as a space for wool-spinning, and finally as a dwelling. William Spence, a young Scotsman who was head gardener at the Mansion House Farm in 1799, probably lived here. Washington hired European-trained gardeners who could cultivate the varieties of plants and seeds he received from around the world. With the aid of two or three slaves, Spence oversaw the upper and lower gardens, orchard, and greenhouse.

Salt House

This structure (interior shown below) provided secure storage for the large quantities of salt that Washington seasonally imported from England, Portugal, and the Caribbean. Fresh meat and fish were packed in dry salt or brine for preservation. Salting fish was particularly important; herring and shad were plentiful in the Potomac River, providing Washington with income and supplying sustenance for everyone on the plantation.

Spinning Room

Slaves and itinerant weavers worked here to produce basic textiles for use at Mount Vernon. As disputes with England grew, Washington tried to improve the quality of the cloth they made. For the production of more utilitarian textiles, he practiced selective breeding of sheep, grew flax and hemp for making linen cloth and rope, and experimented with cotton and silk. Finer materials for table linens and clothing still had to be ordered from England.

Overseer's Quarters

Each of George Washington's five farms had its own overseer, who supervised livestock and crops and submitted weekly reports. Overseers also managed enslaved and free laborers.

Besides his typical duties, Mansion House Farm overseer Roger Farrell agreed in 1799 to supervise the annual harvest of fish; keep Washington supplied with mutton, lamb, veal, and firewood; and repair fences around the estate, among other tasks. That year, Farrell earned $133.33, plus "board, bed lodging, and washing."

OPPOSITE: *This north lane outbuilding contains the spinning room and the overseer's quarters.*
BELOW: *The interior of the overseer's quarters.*

Blacksmith Shop

The blacksmith shop was essential to the running of the plantation and vital to George Washington's business endeavors. Records indicate that as early as 1755 a blacksmith shop was located along the north lane, about 200 feet from the Mansion. Most of the smiths who worked for Washington were slaves, except for a Dutch (or German) immigrant named Dominicus Gubner.

Most of the tasks performed here were relatively mundane: making nails and hooks, mending well-worn pots and pans, and crafting various farm tools. But Washington also challenged the blacksmith to create a plow he had designed and to make intricate parts for pistols and rifles. In his rare spare time, the blacksmith did small jobs for Washington's neighbors in order to increase the estate's income.

This reconstruction of the blacksmith shop, completed in 2009, is on the site of the original building. An excavation by Mount Vernon's archaeologists, along with period paintings and other primary sources, provided valuable clues about the structure's design. Letters, account ledgers, and other written sources detail the tools Washington purchased to outfit the shop and also indicate the types of repair work done there.

Hardware handcrafted by Mount Vernon's present-day blacksmiths is available for purchase in the gift shops.

Shoemaker's Shop

The shoemaker played a critical role by maintaining the plantation workers' shoes so that no labor or time was lost. Footwear was often purchased from outside manufacturers; one pair of shoes was issued annually to each slave and repaired over the course of the year. The shoemaker, who might have been a hired white artisan or a slave, also worked on saddles and other leather goods. In his later years, Washington's trusted personal servant Billy Lee worked as one of the estate's shoemakers.

Stove Room

The corner fireplace (below right) heated the greenhouse on the opposite side of this building. Hot air from the fire was conducted through flues and channeled under the greenhouse floor to heat the delicate plants and the roots of potted trees (right).

Greenhouse Slave Quarters

A little more than 25 percent (that is, about 85) of Mount Vernon's slaves lived on the Mansion House Farm, either in these quarters, in outbuildings where they worked, or in small cabins nearby. The men's living space is furnished with a range of clothing and implements to suggest their jobs as servants in the Mansion, as craftsmen, and as skilled laborers. Personal items include grooming necessities, such as a razor, soap, a bowl, a brush, and a comb. In the women's room, a spinning wheel, laundry, and knitting items represent the tasks many of them performed. Clothing placed on the bunks and hung from pegs represents the types of garments each woman was allotted annually as well as the better garments provided for female house servants.

Music and storytelling helped establish and preserve the slaves' culture. A jaw harp that archaeologists unearthed at the site of the original blacksmith shop could have been used by either a slave or a white servant. The cellar of an excavated slave quarters also yielded fragments of clay pipes of the kind used by both men and women for smoking tobacco (see page 193). As music and tobacco aroma filled the quarters, some people told stories. A number of Mount Vernon's slaves came from Africa, and as an adult, Martha Washington's grandson George Washington (Washy) Parke Custis remembered hearing one of them reminisce:

> *Father Jack was an African negro, an hundred years of age, and, although greatly enfeebled in body by such a vast weight of years, his mind possessed uncommon vigor. And he would tell of days long past, of Afric's clime, and of Afric's wars, in which he (of course the son of a king) was made captive, and of the terrible battle in which his royal sire was slain, the village consigned to the flames, and he to the slaveship.*

"I can only say that there is not a man living who wishes more sincerely than I do, to see a plan adopted for the abolition of [slavery]; but there is only one proper and effectual mode by which it can be accomplished, and that is by Legislative authority; and this, as far as my suffrage will go, shall never be wanting."

—George Washington to Robert Morris, April 12, 1786

Seen in the men's bunk room are shaving items and ornate shoe buckles of the type worn by Mount Vernon's house servants.

This view of the women's bunk room in the greenhouse slave quarters shows typical clothing, bedding, and other items that saw daily use.

MANSION GROUNDS

By 1799, the last year of Washington's life, Mount Vernon was an 8,000-acre plantation divided into five farms, four of them devoted to agriculture. The fifth, the part visitors see today, was the Mansion House Farm, the site of Washington's home and the groves, gardens, and walkways surrounding it. This farm was also the center of his extended business operations and home to dozens of enslaved, indentured, and hired laborers and craftspeople whose work supported the household and plantation.

Washington spent nearly all of his 45 years as master of Mount Vernon improving the estate and realizing his vision of a gracious home and grounds. He took great care with all the details of his house, grounds, and businesses, overseeing them personally while he was at home and by letter when he was away during the Revolutionary War and his presidency.

"No estate in United America is more pleasantly situated than this," he wrote. "It lyes in a high, dry & healthy country, 300 miles by water from the Sea . . . on one of the finest Rivers in the world."

His care was obvious to visitors from the moment they arrived. People approaching Mount Vernon on horseback or by carriage first saw the house from the west, across a half-mile-long "visto," or view, created by pruning and cutting trees in the outlying woods. Coming nearer, they reached the gate at the bottom of the bowling green and looked up to see the elegant Mansion—framed by two serpentine walks, beds full of plantings, and thick groves of trees. Today's visitors see that very same scene, although the trees are, of course, much taller now.

Washington loved to garden, and the skills he acquired as a surveyor—his initial profession—enabled him to pursue ambitious plans. His first design for the grounds was fairly formal, a quality still evident in the symmetry of the layout. In 1760 he obtained a copy of an influential book by English writer and designer Batty Langley, *New Principles of Gardening* (1728), which inspired him to turn Mount Vernon into a showplace of naturalistic landscaping.

He began extensive work on the land and outbuildings around the Mansion before the Revolutionary War and never let the project languish, despite his eight-year absence and wartime shortages and disruptions. By the time he finished, about 1787, he had replaced many outbuildings, relocated lanes and roads, leveled and expanded lawns, and reshaped the gardens.

What to look for

HA-HA WALLS: Sunken brick walls enclosing the east lawn (opposite top) and flanking the bowling-green gate formed a physical barrier—keeping the farm animals from wandering into the family living area—while also preserving the view. Legend has it that the walls got their name from people who stumbled upon them, unaware they were there.

LANES: Washington laid out two lanes to the north and south of the Mansion. This enabled him to retain the symmetry of his design while keeping the outbuildings, such as the smokehouse, spinning room, and wash house, largely out of view.

MANSION CIRCLE: Washington created a formal courtyard on the west side of the Mansion. At its center is a large ellipse, its precise layout reflective of his surveying skill. By circling the ellipse, carriages could bring visitors directly to the door, and then easily continue around and head toward the stable.

ORIGINAL TREES: Washington collected and planted hundreds of trees, often searching his nearby lands for the best specimens. A few of the larger trees on the bowling green are originals, planted under his direction in 1785.

"The [General] has never left America. [But] after seeing his house and his gardens one would say that he had seen the most beautiful examples in England of this style."

—Julian Niemcewicz,
a Polish visitor to Mount Vernon, June 2, 1798

The "Vaughan Plan"

English amateur architect Samuel Vaughan visited Mount Vernon in the summer of 1787. He explored the estate, took detailed measurements of the Mansion and its immediate surroundings, created this large drawing, and presented it to his friend George Washington. The bird's-eye view delineates major elements of Washington's "pleasure grounds," with a lettered key identifying landscape features. Seen at top are the curving Potomac River and the expansive east lawn. Groves of trees, planted irregularly, flank the Mansion. The formal geometry of the Mansion circle and the straight lines of outbuildings and garden pathways contrast strongly with the serpentine walks that border the central bowling green.

Known today as the "Vaughan Plan," this view captures Washington's "grand design" for the core area of his estate. Preserved among his papers after his death, the drawing descended among family members until it was acquired by Mount Vernon in 1975. It has provided invaluable documentation about the estate's appearance in Washington's day, guiding the restoration of landscape elements that had disappeared over time.

BELOW: *Attributed to Edward Savage and dated about 1787–92, this is one of the two earliest-known views of the house and grounds and captures the bustle of everyday life at Washington's estate.*

Livestock

Washington bred livestock to provide strong work animals as well as wool, leather, meat, milk, butter, and—perhaps most important to a farmer—fertilizer. No part of the animal went to waste: even bones and horns were used for buttons, shoehorns, toothbrushes, and eating utensils. A creative and experimental farmer, Washington was more enthusiastic about animal husbandry than many of his 18th-century peers. Most colonial planters did not breed nearly the number and variety of livestock that populated Mount Vernon. Today's visitors see some of the same breeds that were common two centuries ago, including Ossabaw Island hogs, Hog Island sheep, Bronze turkeys, Dominique chickens, and red Milking Devon cattle.

Livestock breeds on the estate include (clockwise from right): Ossabaw Island hogs, Dominique chickens, draft mules, and Hog Island sheep.

Forest Trail

The forest trail meanders through one of the small woodlands left on the estate, giving visitors a feel for the natural setting of Mount Vernon when George Washington lived here. During his time, only about 3,200 acres of the estate were cultivated. He purposely left most of his land wooded because the forest helped sustain the estate. Trees provided wood for fuel and building. Some plants provided medicine, such as witch hazel to reduce inflammation, sassafras bark for treating fevers, and bloodroot for skin cancers. The wild game inhabiting the forest appeared often on Mount Vernon's dining tables. Washington and his guests also took advantage of the forest for exercise and entertainment. Some of them were avid foxhunters, with Washington perhaps the most enthusiastic of all.

Today, the forest trail winds through a woodland very different from the semi-wilderness Washington knew. Some wildlife has disappeared entirely, while other species of animals that the Washingtons would not have known thrive here. Black bears no longer roam the hills. Tamer creatures, however, such as house finches, European starlings, and a turtle called the red-eared slider, have been introduced to the area over the past two centuries. The canopy of trees has changed, too. Visitors still see the oak and hickory trees that dominated the forest in Washington's day, but the American chestnuts common in 1799 were felled by blight in the 20th century.

What to look for

COBBLE QUARRY: This area was likely a source of stone for the Mount Vernon estate. Cobbles of all sizes were collected and used to construct roadways. Nearby, Washington discovered an outcropping of sandstone, which provided larger blocks for major building projects and may have been used to form the foundation for the first phase of Mansion construction, in 1735.

LIKELY SITE OF A NATIVE AMERICAN HUNTING CAMP: On one of the hilltops along the trail, archaeologists have excavated various Indian artifacts, including stone tools, stone flakes produced from tool making, and fire-cracked rocks from campfire cooking. For thousands of years before the Washington family acquired this land, in 1674, Native Americans lived here. One of the highest points of land in the area, this could well have been the site of a seasonal hunting camp.

GARDENS

Washington's passion for gardens is expressed in the order and variety of those he established at Mount Vernon. He was ever on the lookout for beautiful or interesting specimens, such as the redbud and dogwood trees he saw during his travels to the Virginia piedmont and the mountain laurel he loved for its pink flowers and sculpted foliage.

Although slaves did much of the labor, supervised by hired gardeners, Washington worked, too. One surprised guest observed him throwing off his coat to dig and plant.

Over the years, he developed five different gardens at Mount Vernon. The first—the landscape garden—included the bowling green and its surrounding serpentine walks, which visitors see as they approach the Mansion.

The other four gardens were essential to the estate because of the vegetables, fruits, and herbs they produced:

- the upper garden (see opposite), which included a greenhouse and eventually evolved into a formal pleasure garden;
- the lower garden, which served mainly as the kitchen garden;
- the botanical garden, where Washington experimented with new plants; and
- the fruit garden and nursery, which contained fruit trees and assorted plantings of grass crops, greens, and vegetables.

The lushly colorful upper garden features large square beds abundantly planted with vegetables and bordered by a profusion of flowers and boxwood.

Upper Garden

Washington finished enclosing the walls of the upper garden—his showplace—in 1776. Created as a fruit-and-nuts garden, it was transformed from a garden of necessity to a more decorative one in 1785. Its dominant features are a greenhouse, two formal boxwood parterres, and large beds of vegetables bordered with flowers and boxwood.

Garden Houses

The octagonal structures at the west end of the upper and lower gardens were tool rooms and seed houses. These provided sheltered workspaces for gardeners, who cultivated new plants, gathered their seeds, and carefully stored them. The loss of a single season's seeds could mean the elimination of a prized plant.

ABOVE: *A copper watering pot used at Mount Vernon in the 18th century.* LEFT: *A flower bed along an upper-garden path. Seeds and tools were stored in the nearby garden house.*

Lower Garden

This area was used as the kitchen garden throughout the Washingtons' years at Mount Vernon. It had brick walls for protection and warmth, terracing for level gardening, and espaliered pears and apples along the walks that provided a windbreak for vegetables. The garden supplied much of the essential produce for the family kitchen, including head vegetables such as lettuce, broccoli, cabbage, and cauliflower and herbs such as dill and chives. As plantation mistress, Martha Washington was responsible for this garden, and called the abundance of vegetables "the best part of our living in the country."

Botanical Garden

Between the upper garden and north lane and behind the spinning house lies the small enclosed area where Washington probably spent more time gardening on his own than anywhere else on the estate. In 1785, for instance, he sowed flowering shrubs and ornamentals, experimental hedging plants, nuts, fruits, herbs, new grains, and grasses. He marked the planting locations with notched sticks, watered and mulched, and kept careful notes of the results.

Although Washington was a renowned farmer, often offering advice to and trading seeds with his neighbors, some of his experiments went awry. For instance, in that 1785 planting, he carefully sowed a precious gift: the seeds of 200 Chinese species. The next year, he reported, "None . . . were [to] be seen."

Greenhouse

Completed in 1787, the greenhouse—at the time an unusual feature on the American landscape—allowed Washington to nurture tropical and semitropical plants. Lemon and orange trees and sago palms grew here, much to the delight of strolling guests. An ambitious structure for its day, the greenhouse had many windows to capture the southern sun, a vaulted ceiling that promoted air circulation, and an ingenious heating system that generated radiant heat from a series of flues under the floor. Washington's greenhouse burned in 1835, and the present structure was built in 1951 on the original foundation and based on drawings of the original structure. The reconstruction incorporates bricks from the White House, which was fully renovated between 1948 and 1952.

Fruit Garden and Nursery

This area (below right) began as an experimental vineyard, but, as in most early American vineyards, a soil disease killed the European grape-root stock. After Washington's landscape alterations in 1785, some of the upper garden's fruit trees were transplanted here and laid out in squares, including pears, cherries, peaches, and apples. In this enclosure, Washington also situated a nursery where he grew trees, shrubs, berries, vegetables, and grasses.

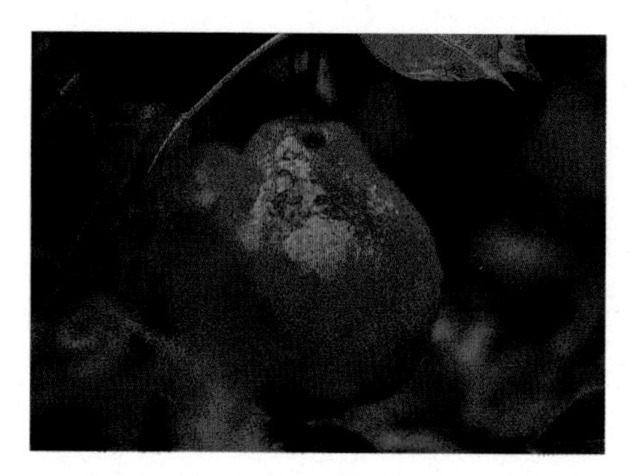

Washington's greenhouse, seen from the upper-garden gate.

TOMB

George Washington left specific instructions for his burial. Because the family vault at Mount Vernon was deteriorating and not "properly situated," he wanted a new one built—of brick and on a larger scale—adjacent to his fruit garden and nursery. In the new vault, he wrote in his will, "my remains, with those of my deceased relatives (now in the old Vault) and such others of my family as may chuse to be entombed there, may be deposited."

Washington's wishes were not immediately heeded. Just after his death, Congress resolved that a marble monument to him should be erected in the new U.S. Capitol building and that the first president's remains should be interred there. Martha Washington's consent was sought and obtained, and a crypt was provided under the Capitol dome. But the project was never completed. In 1831 Washington's surviving executors moved his and Martha's bodies and those of other family members from the old tomb to the present enclosure.

The marble sarcophagus in which Washington's remains now rest was carved in 1837 by John Struthers of Philadelphia. At that time, the lead inner casket was removed from the closed vault and entombed within the marble. A similar sarcophagus, more plainly sculpted, was provided for Mrs. Washington.

The marble obelisks in front of the tomb were erected in memory of the president's nephew Bushrod Washington, his great-nephew John Augustine Washington II, and his great-great nephew John Augustine Washington III, who, in turn, were proprietors of Mount Vernon. Their remains lie in the inner vault along with those of 23 other family members. The memorials on the side of the enclosure mark the graves of Washington's step-granddaughter Eleanor (Nelly) Parke Custis Lewis, her youngest daughter, Mary Eliza Angela Lewis Conrad, and Mary Eliza's infant daughter, Angela.

John Struthers of Philadelphia carved George Washington's marble sarcophagus in 1837.

SLAVE BURIAL GROUND AND MEMORIALS

The slave burial ground near the Tomb was one of several on the plantation. The bodies of slaves who worked on the Mansion House Farm were laid to rest here, on a quiet wooded hillside above the Potomac.

Slaves were buried in coffins made on the plantation. Although there are no markers, ground-penetrating radar indicates the presence of 50 to 75 graves, oriented on an east-west axis. While this is the customary Western model for placing bodies, a tradition in the local African-American community is that the bodies were laid this way so they could face toward Africa—symbolizing a desire to return home.

What to look for

SLAVE MEMORIALS: In 1929 the Mount Vernon Ladies' Association erected a modest memorial to slaves buried on the estate—the first of its kind in the nation. It remained the cemetery's only marker until 1983, when a more formal and substantial memorial was dedicated. Designed by architecture students from Howard University in Washington, D.C., it features a granite shaft in the center of a small circular plaza. The words Love, Hope, and Faith—drawn from biblical scriptures that helped sustain African Americans in slavery—are inscribed on the memorial's steps.

OPPOSITE: *The Slave Memorial Commemoration Ceremony is conducted in the fall by Black Women United for Action and the Mount Vernon Ladies' Association.*

PIONEER FARM

Located on the banks of the Potomac near the wharf, the four-acre Pioneer Farm explores George Washington's role as visionary farmer and represents the more than 3,000 acres he cultivated during the second half of the 18th century. It also offers visitors a chance to learn more about the lives of Mount Vernon field slaves who put his agrarian ideas into practice.

Washington used Mount Vernon as a laboratory for testing and implementing progressive farming methods. For example, in the mid-1760s, he became one of the first large-scale Virginia planters to switch his main cash crop from tobacco—traditionally a staple of the colony's economy—to wheat. At the same time, he began experimenting with composting and crop rotation as well as with more efficient designs for basic farming tools such as the barrel plow and various harrows.

Washington's life as a farmer sheds light on his struggle with one of the most difficult facts of his day: slavery. Although he eventually opposed the institution, his five farms relied on the labor of more than 300 enslaved people. Over time, Washington resisted the harshest punishments, resolved not to buy or sell any more slaves, and refused to break up families. Yet the 132 enslaved field workers at Mount Vernon when he died—most of them women—performed the backbreaking work of clearing, plowing, planting, and harvesting.

At the Pioneer Farm, which is most active from April through October, visitors can see the 16-sided treading barn Washington designed and the re-created cabin similar to those inhabited by families of field hands. Various demonstrations are conducted throughout the season, following Washington's agricultural calendar. Visitors can observe tasks the slaves did being performed, such as hoeing the fields, cracking corn, and winnowing wheat. Sheep, mules, horses, and oxen work on the site, and costumed interpreters explain some of Washington's agricultural techniques, such as his seven-year crop-rotation plan.

The site is a 15-minute walk from the Mansion. It is also accessible via a shuttle bus that runs continuously between the Donald W. Reynolds Museum and Education Center and the farm. For more information on each day's activities and the bus schedule, inquire at the Ford Orientation Center information desk.

ABOVE: *Slaves Silla and Slamin Joe greet Washington at their cabin during one of the estate's character-interpretation programs.* OPPOSITE: *Washington's innovative design for his 16-sided treading barn included this intricate geometric ceiling.*

What to look for

BARN: One of Washington's masterful farming innovations was a 16-sided barn designed for treading wheat—his most important cash crop. Traditionally, wheat was threshed by hand, a slow and arduous process of beating the wheat to break the grain out of the straw. Sometimes horses treaded wheat by trampling it on the ground, but that practice was unsanitary and exposed the grain to weather. Washington decided to move the threshing process indoors and began, in 1793, to have the barn built; it was completed two years later. Horses trotted in a circle on the second floor, treading on grain that fell to the first floor through narrow gaps in the flooring. Although Washington was in Philadelphia serving as president while the barn was under construction, he supervised the work from afar. He even calculated (correctly) that the number of bricks needed to complete the first floor would be 30,820. The barn at the Pioneer Farm is an exact replica of the original, based on careful examination of Washington's drawings and plans from the 1790s as well as on a mid-19th-century photograph showing the barn in a semi-ruined state (above).

This is a photograph of the 16-sided treading barn, which originally stood about three miles from the Mansion on Washington's Dogue Run Farm and is thought to have been demolished sometime after 1870.

SLAVE CABIN: This reproduction building shows the conditions under which most Mount Vernon slaves lived. The wooden cabin recalls the home of a family who lived at Washington's Dogue Run Farm. The father, Slamin Joe, was a ditch digger who slept in the slave quarters near the Mansion, returning home for visits on Sundays. His wife, Priscilla (Silla), was a field hand. The couple had six children. The whole family occupied the sparsely furnished cabin.

Firsthand accounts indicate that the cabins were sparsely furnished and that the adults slept on a bed described as a "mean-pallet." A small table and some cooking utensils as well as some clothing and blankets would be present. The floor was clay, and the hearth provided the family with a cooking area, heat, and light.

POTOMAC RIVER.

THE WHARF AND POTOMAC RIVER

In the 18th century, waterways like the Potomac River were major travel and commerce routes and provided critical natural resources. George Washington shipped and received countless goods via the river and transported crops around his large estate on both the Potomac and nearby Dogue Creek. In addition to its value as a trade route, the river supplied Washington with one of his most important commodities: fish. In 1772 alone, his fisheries reaped 1.3 million herring and more than 11,000 shad. Those harvests helped feed the Mount Vernon plantation and provided an important source of income.

The wharf was rebuilt in 1880, replacing an earlier structure, during a time when most visitors arrived at Mount Vernon by boat. The wharf was restored in 1991 and dedicated that year by Her Majesty Queen Elizabeth II of Great Britain.

Learn more about the river—and how Washington used it—on the display located at the wharf.

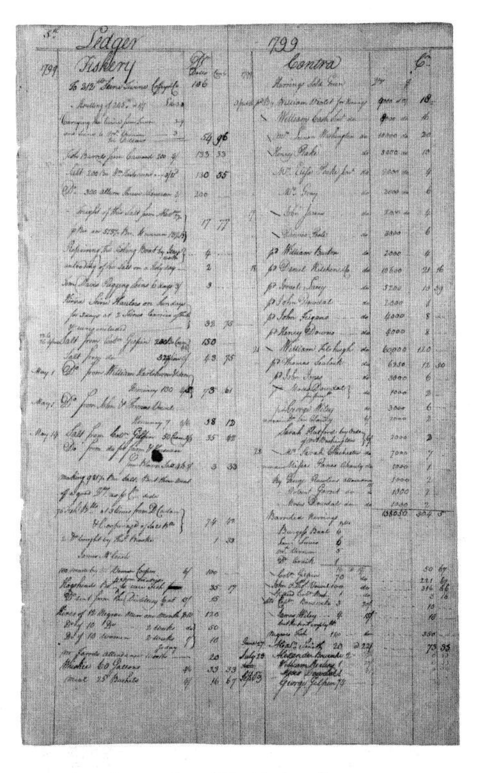
Ledger 1799
Fishery
Contra

ABOVE: *A page from Washington's 1799 accounts ledger for his fishery at Mount Vernon.* LEFT: *His fishing-tackle box, on view in the Museum.* OPPOSITE: *The wharf today (top) and a 19th-century view of it from the river (bottom).*

EDUCATION
RECONSTRUCTING
GEORGE WASHINGTO

DONALD W. REYNOLDS MUSEUM AND EDUCATION CENTER

Opened in 2006, the Museum and Education Center was made possible by the Donald W. Reynolds Foundation, the most generous benefactor in Mount Vernon's history. This state-of-the-art facility provides visitors with a compelling experience while introducing them to the real George Washington.

Entering the building, visitors see on their right a decorative and fine arts museum featuring objects from the Washingtons' personal life. To the left is an interactive education center, with displays devoted to Washington's military exploits and triumphs as a political leader, among other highlights.

The corridor to the far left features a gallery focused on the rescue and restoration of Mount Vernon; it leads to the Mount Vernon Inn Complex and to the exit.

Museum Highlights

The Museum displays artifacts and features temporary exhibitions focused on a range of Washington-related topics. Highlights include:

PRESIDENTIAL MEAL: A presidential-dining scenario depicts one of the meals Washington hosted every Thursday afternoon at 4 p.m. at his residence in Philadelphia, which was the U.S. capital in the 1790s. Congressmen and other government officials were invited to dine with him and Mrs. Washington, who often was the only woman present. The table setting includes French porcelain dishes and figures, a mirrored centerpiece, and blue glass finger bowls.

This Chinese porcelain platter saw everyday use on the Washingtons' dining table.

Donald W. Reynolds Museum and Education Center Floor Plans

EDUCATION CENTER

A Reconstructing George Washington
B Young Virginian
C Young Surveyor
D Upstart Colonial Officer
E Gentleman Planter
F *A 40-Year Romance* Theater
G Becoming a Revolutionary
H First in War
I Revolutionary War Theater
J Citizen Soldier
K Hands-on-History Center
L Visionary Enterpreneur
M The Dilemma of Slavery
N A Leader's Smile
O Indispensable American
P The People's President
Q Setting Precedents
R Private Citizen
S Legacy Theater
T Saving Mount Vernon

MUSEUM

- A Houdon Bust
- B The World of Washington
- C From Soldier to Statesman
- D At Home with the Washingtons
- E The Washington Style
- F Books and Manuscripts
- G Temporary Exhibitions

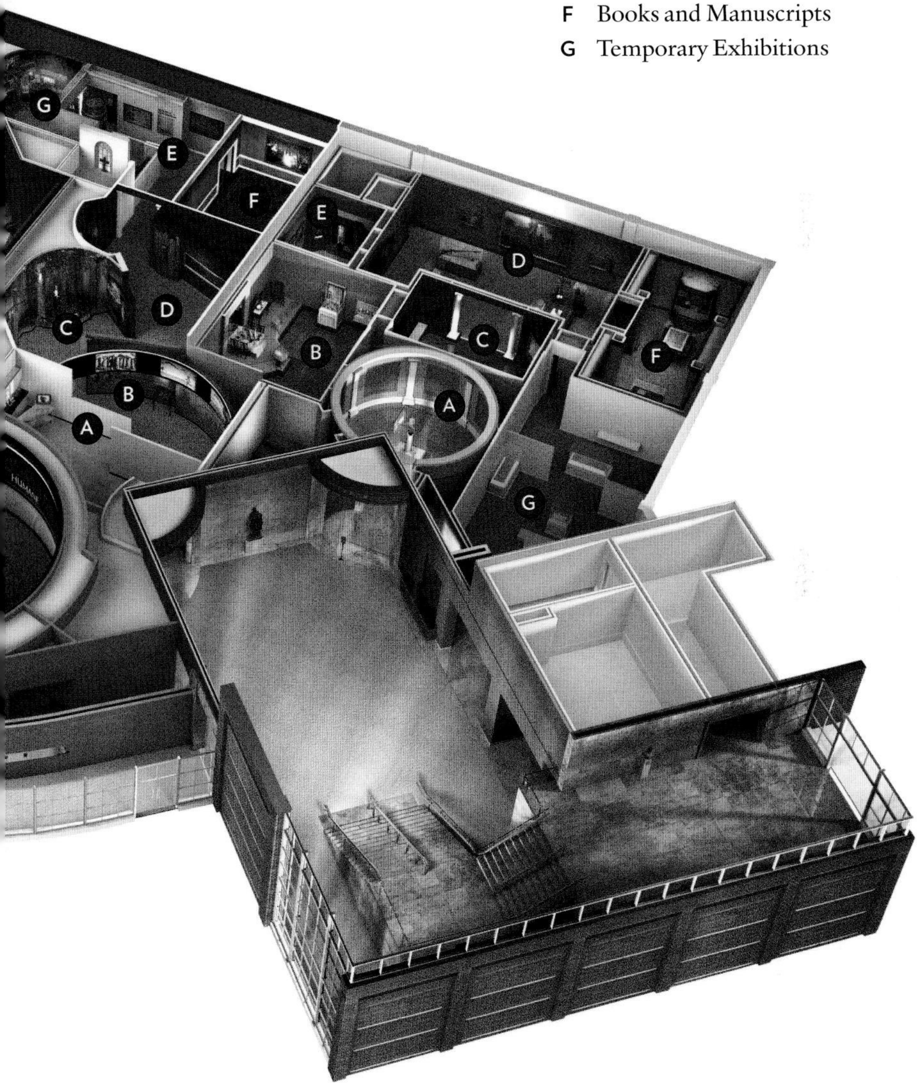

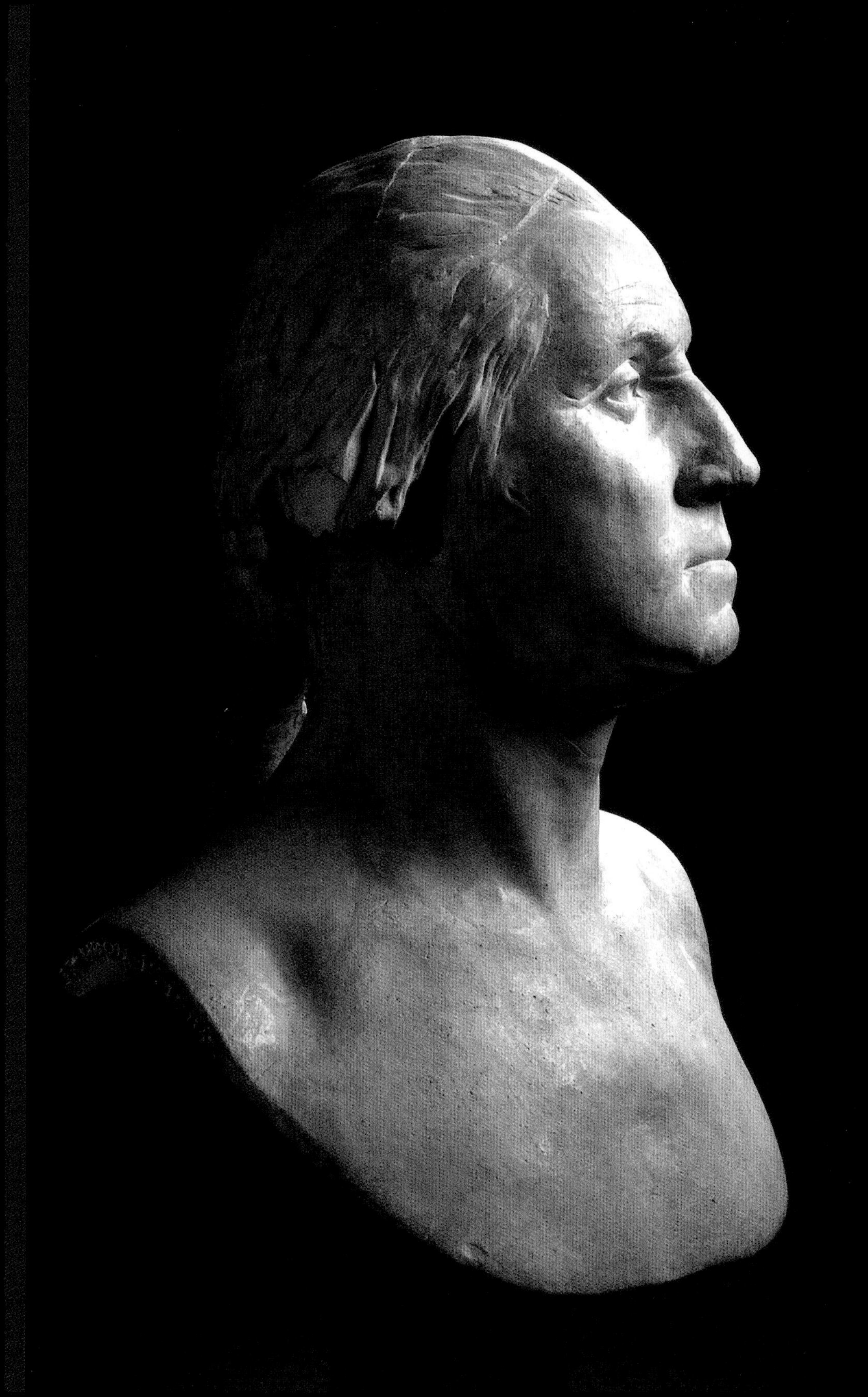

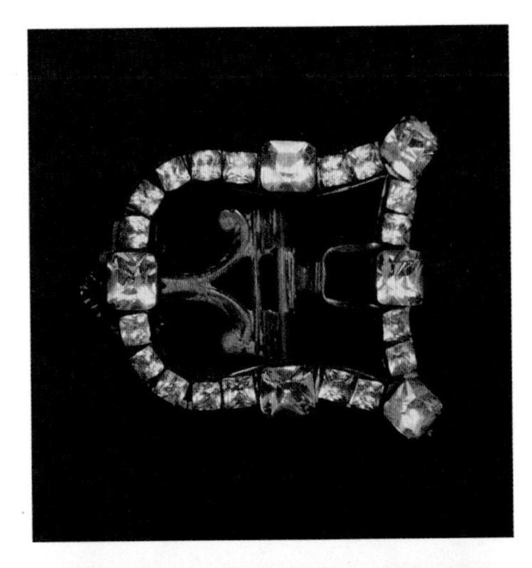

HOUDON BUST: Jean-Antoine Houdon's 1785 clay bust of Washington is perhaps Mount Vernon's most prized artifact. This sculpture, the most accurate likeness of the man ever created, is installed at Washington's height to give visitors a sense of his commanding presence.

CLOTHING ACCESSORIES: George and Martha Washington favored sophisticated but understated adornments, such as the shoe and knee buckles the general wore and Mrs. Washington's earrings and necklaces. Washington understood how the objects he selected and displayed could communicate the spirit of American independence and the standing of the young republic.

TOP: *Martha Washington's fashionable waist buckle, set with artificial stones.* LEFT: *George Washington's topaz-encrusted knee and shoe buckles.* BOTTOM RIGHT: *Mrs. Washington's garnet earrings.* BOTTOM LEFT: *Her seed-pearl dove pin.*

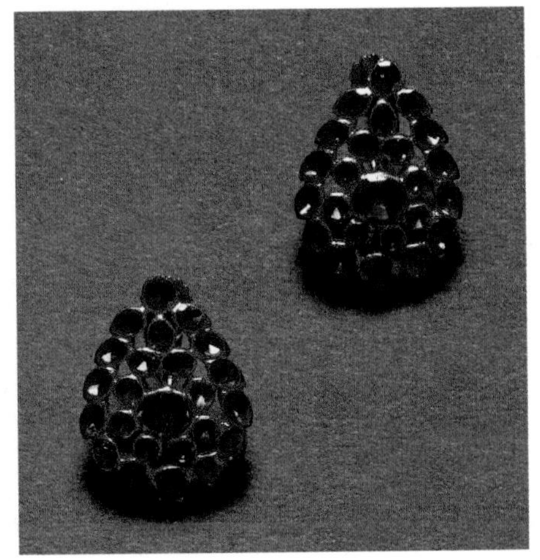

LAST WILL AND TESTAMENT: In this 29-page document (see opposite), Washington penned his last wishes. He freed his own slaves and made provisions for the support of those who could not care for themselves. He also left money to establish a school for orphans in Alexandria. Martha Washington was given the use of his estate for the remainder of her life. Washington stipulated that, after her death, his property should be split up among his large extended family. Nephew Bushrod Washington inherited the Mansion and surrounding land. Pages are on view on a rotating basis, courtesy of the Fairfax County, Virginia, circuit court.

SPURS: In the first months at Valley Forge, during the winter of 1777–78, Congress wanted the Continental Army to commandeer what it needed from civilians. Washington, however, was unwilling to risk turning the American people against his army. According to words inscribed on these silver spurs, Washington took them from his boots and gave them to Lieutenant Thomas Lamb (who had no spurs) with orders to ride to Boston to retrieve much-needed supplies. The spurs are displayed along with Washington's sword and silver camp cups (see page 174).

GLOBE: Washington ordered this globe, which formerly sat in his study, from London. He used it during his presidency and later at Mount Vernon. The object reflects his desire to increase his understanding of the world around him. His awareness of the wider world no doubt prompted one of his significant accomplishments as president: keeping the young nation out of foreign entanglements.

In the na[illegible] of God amen

I George Washington of Mount Vernon—a citi[illegible] of the United States, —and lately Pr[illegible]ident of the same, do make, ord[illegible] and declare this Instrument, [illegible] is written with my own hand, [illegible] every page there of subscribed [illegible] my name, to be my last Will & [illegible]tament, revo-king all other[illegible]

Imprimis. All m[illegible] [illegible]ts, of which there are but few, and none of magnitude, are to be punctu[illegible] and speedily paid —and the legac[illegible] hereafter bequeath-ed, are to be dis[illegible]ged as soon as cir-cumstances will [illegible]mit, and in the manner directe[illegible]

Item. To my dea[illegible] [illegible]oved wife Mar-tha Washington [illegible] give and bequeath the use, profit [illegible] benefit of my whole Estate, real an[illegible] [illegible]al; for the ter[illegible] of her natura[illegible]

10

Patronize the measure, and the Divi-dends proceeding from the purchase of such Stock is to be vested in more Stock, and so on, until a sum ade-quate to the accomplishment of the object is obtained, of which I have not the smallest doubt, before many years passes away, even if no aid or encouraged is given by Legisla-tive authority, or from any other source

Item The hundred shares which I held in the James River Company, I have gi-ven, and now confirm in perpetuity to, and for the use & benefit of Li-berty-Hall Academy, in the County of Rockbridge, in the Commonwealth of Virga

Item I release exonerate and discharge the Estate of my deceased brother Sam-uel Washington, from the payment of the money which is due to me for the Land I sold to Philip Pendleton (lying in the County of Berkeley) who assigned the same to him the said Sam-uel; who, by agreement was to pay me therefor. — And Whereas by some contract (the purport of which was never communicated to me) between the said Samuel and his son Thorn-ton Washington, the latter became pos-sessed of the aforesaid Land, without

G Washington

ELIZABETH AND STANLEY DEFOREST SCOTT GALLERY
Riding Crop

Among the Museum's highlights are George Washington's hunting horn and the original painted-metal dove of peace that crowned the weathervane atop the Mansion.

Education Center Highlights

The interactive Education Center tells the story of George Washington's life, with an emphasis on the events of his wartime service and presidency. Highlights include:

DIORAMA: Much of what Washington learned about military tactics and strategy he acquired through trial and error. A diorama of the battle at Fort Necessity (detail, right) depicts one of his early military mistakes—from which he learned a great deal.

SCULPTURE: Located at the entrance to the Education Center is a large counter-relief sculpture of Washington's head (opposite), specially lit so that its gaze seems to follow visitors around the room.

SPYMASTER VIDEO: George Washington often used coded messages, invisible ink, and an impressive network of secret agents during the Revolutionary War. A brief video provides an overview of his critical role as a successful and skilled American spymaster.

SWORD: Washington carried this silver-hilted sword (below) during the French and Indian War, when he demonstrated conspicuous bravery under fire. Now bare, the wooden grip was originally wrapped with spiraling bands of silver tape and twisted silver wire.

Theaters

The 10-minute film *A 40-Year Romance* is shown in a room decorated as an 18th-century parlor. It highlights George and Martha Washington's courtship along with major events in their 40-year marriage, as told from Martha's perspective and narrated by actress Glenn Close.

Presented in the Revolutionary War Theater (right) is a fast-paced, 14-minute multimedia production tracing three military engagements: Boston, Trenton, and Yorktown. The combination of narration and sensory effects helps evoke a sense of actual conditions and events. For instance, when the audience hears cannon fire, the seats rumble and smoke drifts through the theater. And when the American troops cross the Delaware River, "snow" falls from overhead.

Screened in the Legacy Theater is a four-minute patriotic finale summarizing Washington's contributions to the nation. Featured are the voices of Pulitzer Prize–winning historian David McCullough, former U.S. Secretary of State Colin Powell, and the award-winning Brooklyn Youth Chorus.

SCOVERING THE REAL
A LEADER OF CHARACTER

WHISKEY STILL: Washington was an innovative farmer and able entrepreneur. His diverse business portfolio included extensive farms, a substantial fishery, and a cutting-edge gristmill and distillery. On display is an early 19th-century still like those used in Washington's profitable distillery (center right and page 161).

DRESS AND SLIPPERS: When the widow Martha Dandridge Custis married George Washington in 1759, she was a vibrant 27-year-old. A reproduction of her wedding dress and slippers are displayed (left).

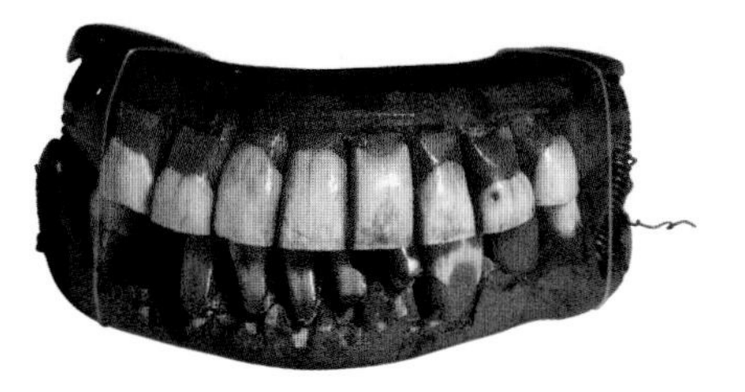

DENTURES: Visitors are immediately drawn to Washington's dentures (left), an exceptionally personal and evocative artifact. From losing two teeth during the French and Indian War to receiving his last set of dentures, in 1798, Washington suffered dental problems throughout his adult life.

COFFIN: The nation mourned when George Washington died suddenly, on December 14, 1799. A reproduction coffin (below), which was made for the commemoration of the 200th anniversary of his death, sits atop an original 18th-century bier in a display detailing his final hours.

FORENSIC MODELS: Using a variety of sources and artifacts, a team of forensic scientists painstakingly determined what Washington looked like at three key ages. The lifelike and life-sized figures on display in the Education Center represent him at 19, 45, and 57.

OATH OF OFFICE: Standing on the second-floor balcony of Federal Hall in New York City, Washington took the oath of office before an adoring crowd. Place your hand on an interactive Bible, and repeat the words he spoke during his inauguration.

Three forensic models of George Washington depict him as the 19-year-old surveyor (top), 45-year-old general at Valley Forge (bottom left), and 57-year-old first U.S. president (bottom right).

PRESIDENTIAL OATH OF OFFICE
TAKING THE OATH
STEPPING INTO HISTORY
1789

GEORGE WASHINGTON'S DISTILLERY & GRISTMILL

Two of the best embodiments of Washington's business acumen are located a little less than three miles from the estate. Long before his death, the gristmill had proven to be one of his most profitable ventures; flour produced there reached markets as far away as the West Indies, England, and southern Europe. The distillery was an immediate success, and by 1799 it was one of the largest producers of whiskey in the United States.

After years of painstaking archaeological research and reconstruction, the two buildings stand in a charming creek-side location, looking much as they did in 1799.

An early 19th-century copper whiskey still, on view in the Education Center. TOP LEFT: *The reconstructed distillery.* BOTTOM LEFT: *Artist Lee Boynton's 2010 depiction of the busy distillery and gristmill complex as it might have appeared in the summer of 1799.*

Distillery

In 1797 Washington's newly hired Scottish farm manager, James Anderson, proposed construction of a whiskey distillery near the gristmill at Dogue Run Farm. Washington was initially hesitant but then agreed to move forward. "[A distillery is] a business I am entirely unacquainted with," he wrote to Anderson that June, "but from your knowledge of it and from the confidence you have in the profit to be derived from the establishment, I am disposed to enter upon one."

The first distilling was done using two copper-pot stills installed in the cooperage next to the gristmill. The 600 gallons made sold very well and yielded a good profit. Washington then agreed to build a new facility that would contain five stills. In 1798, the first year it operated, the larger distillery produced 4,500 gallons of rye whiskey. The following year, production rose to nearly 11,000 gallons.

It took a team of eight to keep the new distillery running. James Anderson's son, master distiller John Anderson, produced the alcohol with the help of one assistant and six slaves.

What to look for

MASH TUBS: The chief beverage made at the distillery was rye whiskey, based on a recipe combining 60 percent rye, 35 percent corn, and 5 percent malted barley. The grains were ground at the gristmill and then cooked and fermented at the distillery in large barrels, called mash tubs. As hot water was added from the boiler, enslaved workers would stir in the grains. The starches in the grains were converted into sugars, and yeast was added to turn the sugars into alcohol. Distillery work was exhausting: standing in a room made oppressively hot by the fires used to heat the water, workers ceaselessly stirred the mash, a liquid that started out with the consistency of oatmeal and only gradually became thinner.

REPLICA STILLS: After fermenting from three to five days, the liquid was moved from the mash tubs into a copper-pot still. It was double distilled to produce a drink of about 80 to 90 proof, known as common whiskey. Some whiskey was distilled three or four times to yield a higher-potency alcohol—sometimes called rectified whiskey—that may have been 120 proof. The five replica stills on display here range in size from 70 to 92 gallons, smaller than the 110-to-135-gallon stills of Washington's time. The replicas, like the originals, are made of solid copper. Copper is not only a good conductor of heat, but its use in stills also allows impurities such as sulphur to be separated from the distilled spirits.

BARRELS: After being distilled, the whiskey was stored in 31-gallon oak barrels—typically made by Washington's own coopers—until the drink was purchased. In Washington's day, whiskey typically was not aged, and barrels were simply a means of transporting the spirits to market.

EXHIBITS: The second floor features the distiller's office and living quarters; a video produced by The History Channel, *George Washington's Liquid Gold*; and a permanent exhibit, *Spirits of Independence: George Washington and the Beginnings of the American Whiskey Industry*.

ACCOUNT LEDGER: Covering the period 1797–99, the ledger documents the distillery's transactions and records the various whiskies sold. The distillery also produced apple and peach brandies, some of which likely were imbibed by the Washingtons and their guests. The inventory taken soon after Washington died indicates that cinnamon whiskey, persimmon brandy, peach brandy, and apple brandy, along with whiskey, were stored in the Mansion's basement.

Visiting the Distillery & Gristmill

The Distillery & Gristmill are open to visitors from April through October. To reach the site from the estate, follow Mount Vernon Memorial Highway/Route 235 south for 2.7 miles. You will pass Grist Mill Park on the right and Fort Belvoir on the left. The entrance is about two-tenths of a mile past Fort Belvoir, on the right.

Shuttle service between the Donald W. Reynolds Museum and Education Center and the Distillery & Gristmill is offered from April to October.

Gristmill

In 1766 George Washington switched his main cash crop from tobacco to wheat and, four years later, replaced a dilapidated mill on his Dogue Run Farm with a larger and more efficient operation. Flour production for overseas markets provided him with a much more reliable income than tobacco and greater economic freedom. While the tobacco trade was controlled by the British Crown, flour markets were not—so he could ship his product wherever there were willing customers.

The new mill relied on the force of water from Dogue Run, coursing over a 16-foot wheel, to produce the power that turned the millstones. One set of millstones ground corn for use on the plantation; the other processed wheat for sale locally and for foreign export. In 1791 Washington not only repaired the aging mill but also became one of the nation's first mill owners to install a new, more efficient automated-milling system, designed by Oliver Evans of Delaware.

"At present my Mill has the reputation of turning out superfine flour of the first quality; it commands a higher price in this Country & the West Indies than any other."

—George Washington to Robert Lewis and Sons, April 12, 1785

What to look for

OLIVER EVANS MILLING SYSTEM: In 1790 Evans received U.S. Patent No. 3 for his automated system, which included elevators to move grain and flour through the mill free of manual labor. The system also connected all machines in the mill with a series of chutes and spouts, allowing for continuous milling and resulting in greatly increased efficiency. This is the nation's only gristmill with a working Evans system.

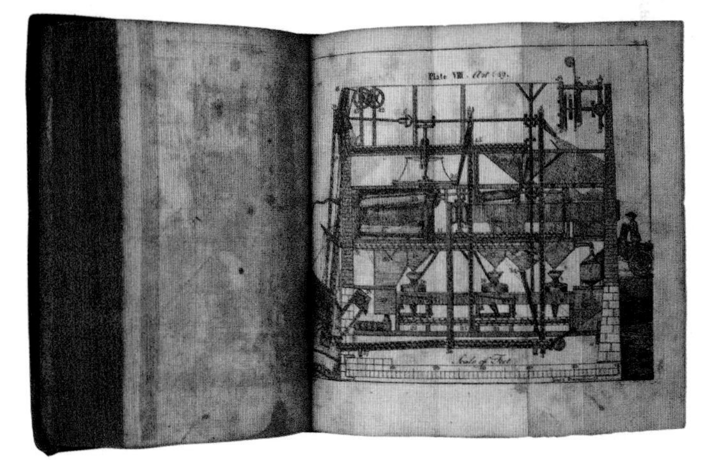

ABOVE: *One of 25 detailed diagrams of milling mechanisms included in Oliver Evans's 1795 book,* The Young Mill-Wright and Miller's Guide. LEFT: *The "hopper boy," a feature of Evans's system, is a mechanized rake that spreads and cools the flour before final sifting.*

MILLSTONES: The reconstructed four-level stone mill accommodates two sets of millstones. Those used for grinding the wheat are French burrstone, a freshwater quartz quarried along the Marne River, not far from Paris. The French stone is extremely hard, with small pits that aid in producing superfine flour and allow air to circulate, reducing the heat of the grinding process. Each stone weighs as much as 2,500 pounds and, with proper maintenance, can last up to 300 years.

Today, the other set of stones in the mill are made of American granite. In Washington's time, the set used for grinding corn and other grains was likely made of a volcanic stone quarried near Cologne, Germany, known as "cullen stones."

WATERWHEEL: Archaeological evidence indicates that the waterwheel in Washington's mill was located inside the building, where visitors see it today.

"I hope, some day or another we shall become a storehouse and granary For the world."

—George Washington to the Marquis de Lafayette, June 18, 1788

The Distillery & Gristmill after Washington's Death

After Washington died, Lawrence Lewis, husband of Martha Washington's granddaughter Nelly, briefly operated the distillery and gristmill. By 1804, James and John Anderson had left Mount Vernon, forcing Lewis to seek managers for both facilities.

The last mention of a working distillery was in 1808, when an Alexandria merchant renting the property advertised whiskey for sale. A fire in 1814 destroyed the structure.

Over time, the gristmill fell into disrepair and by the 1850s was dismantled. In 1932 the Commonwealth of Virginia built a reconstruction of the mill, using parts salvaged from a historic mill in the Shenandoah Valley. Mount Vernon assumed management of the site in 1997 and restored the mill to working condition. In 2007, after years of exacting archaeological work and the successful firing of a replica still, Mount Vernon completed its reconstruction of the distillery, supported by members of the Distilled Spirits Council of the U.S. Three years later, employing the same techniques used in the late 1790s, the distillery began producing George Washington Rye Whiskey for sale to the public.

LEFT: *The miller connects the mill's gear with an engagement lever. The double-gear arrangement lets him operate each set of millstones (shown at right) either independently or at the same time.*

Charles Peale Polk's striking portrait George Washington at Princeton *(mid-1790s).* OPPOSITE: *Washington owned numerous swords, including this elaborately engraved one, which he is believed to have worn to his first presidential inauguration, in April 1789.*

Meet
George Washington

TOP TO BOTTOM: *A miniature portrait of Washington by Charles Willson Peale (1776); his silver-tipped riding crop used while hunting, one of his favorite pastimes; his gold pocket watch; and his mahogany-and-brass telescope.*

George Washington was born at his father's plantation on Popes Creek in Westmoreland County in the British colony of Virginia on February 22, 1732. His father, Augustine Washington, was a leading planter in the area. Sometime between 1735 and 1739, the family moved to Ferry Farm, a plantation on the Rappahannock River near Fredericksburg, Virginia, where George spent much of his youth.

Little is known about Washington's childhood—still the least understood chapter of his life. Several popular anecdotes meant to illustrate his youthful honesty, piety, and physical strength have no basis in documented fact. For example, the story that he once threw a silver dollar across the Potomac River—an impossible feat—originated in the recollections of a cousin that George could throw a stone across the much narrower Rappahannock River. Others, including the familiar tale of young George and the cherry tree, apparently were invented by one of his first biographers, Mason Locke Weems.

When George was 11 years old, his father died, leaving most of his property to the boy's older half-brothers, Lawrence and Augustine. As the oldest child remaining at home, George undoubtedly helped his mother, Mary Ball Washington, manage the Rappahannock River plantation, where he learned to value hard work and efficiency.

Like many other wealthy colonial planters, Augustine Washington intended to send his sons to England to finish their schooling. Although George's two older half-brothers enjoyed this advantage, the death of his father made schooling abroad an impossibility for the boy. He may instead have attended a school near his home for a few years and later gone to another one, either in Fredericksburg, Stafford County, or Westmoreland County. He excelled in mathematics and learned surveying, but he was not taught Latin or ancient Greek as many gentlemen's sons were, and he never learned a foreign language. His formal education ended around age fifteen.

Eager for adventure, George wanted to join the British Navy, but his mother refused to let him. Instead, he accompanied George William Fairfax as a surveyor into the unexplored wilderness of the Virginia frontier. To learn the geometric principles necessary for surveying, young George read books on mathematics.

In July 1749, at age 17 and largely through the influence of the Fairfax family, Washington secured an appointment as surveyor for the newly created frontier county of Culpeper. Seeking to establish himself as a member of the gentry class, he worked hard, saved his money, and bought unclaimed land.

Two years after the death in 1752 of his older half-brother Lawrence, Washington began leasing Mount Vernon from Lawrence's widow, Ann. He also took Lawrence's place in the Virginia militia—the first step in his military career—during the French and Indian War. Early in the conflict, Virginia Lieutenant Governor Robert Dinwiddie sent 21-year-old Major Washington to deliver a message to French troops encamped in the Ohio Country, demanding they leave the area. Washington's account of the arduous 900-mile journey was published in both Williamsburg (Virginia's colonial capital) and London, thus establishing his celebrity by the time he was twenty-two. A few months later, Dinwiddie again dispatched Washington, now a lieutenant colonel, and some 150 men to assert Virginia's claims. In this campaign, he and his troops were forced to surrender after a battle at a site called Fort Necessity.

Although he resigned his commission after this defeat, Washington returned to the frontier in 1755 as a volunteer aide to British

General Edward Braddock. During a battle to drive the French from the Ohio Country, Braddock's army was routed near the Monongahela River and fled in confusion to Virginia. Two horses were shot from under Washington, and four bullets pierced his coat. He behaved with conspicuous bravery but could do little except lead the defeated survivors to safety.

In recognition of his heroic conduct, Washington was given command of Virginia's entire military force of a few hundred men. He was ordered to protect a frontier some 350 miles long. In 1758 the British finally took possession of the strategic forks of the Ohio River, where the French had built Fort Duquesne, and in doing so reasserted British control of the region. As peace returned to Virginia, Washington resigned his commission and went home to Mount Vernon.

In January 1759, he married Martha Dandridge Custis, the young widow of Daniel Parke Custis, one of Virginia's wealthiest men. Soon after, settled at Mount Vernon, Washington wrote, "I am now I [believe] fixd at this Seat with an agreeable Consort for Life and hope to find more happiness in retirement than I ever experiencd amidst a wide and bustling World."

In 1761 Washington fully inherited Mount Vernon, following the death of his half-brother Lawrence's widow. He worked tirelessly to improve his estate and to excel as an innovative farmer and a resourceful entrepreneur. Under his stewardship, for instance, Mount Vernon became the center of a large commercial-fishing operation, thanks to its location on the shad- and herring-rich Potomac. He was also an eager real estate investor, acquiring tens of thousands of acres along the western frontier.

ABOVE: *Washington's elegant mahogany dressing table features a hinged top fitted with a mirror.* RIGHT: *This wool suit may well be the one Washington wore to his first presidential inauguration, on April 30, 1789.*

This 1853 engraving by Paul Giradet, after Emanuel Leutze's monumental painting Washington Crossing the Delaware *(1851), shows the general leading his men on Christmas night 1776 toward their successful surprise attack on Hessian troops.* RIGHT: *Two silver camp cups (engraved with Washington's family crest), which he used during the Revolutionary War, and one of his English-made flintlock pistols.*

Rembrandt Peale's heroic 1823 portrait of George Washington.

Martha's inheritance from her first husband increased Washington's wealth and gave him a ready source of money for his lucrative ventures.

Although the couple had no children of their own, they raised Martha's son, John (Jacky) Parke Custis, and daughter, Martha (Patsy) Parke Custis. Washington was actively involved in their upbringing, ordering books, clothes, and toys for them and overseeing their educations. When Patsy died at age 17, probably of epilepsy, he wept at her bedside.

As a man of property and member of the Virginia House of Burgesses, the colony's elected legislative body, Washington was deeply concerned about the growing disputes between Great Britain and its American colonies. In the fall of 1774, as the calls for independence grew louder, Washington's peers, who recognized him as a dependable man of strength and good sense, named him a representative to the Continental Congress. And in June 1775, the Congress commissioned him to take command of the Continental Army. He wrote home to Martha that he expected to return safely to her in the fall. Instead, the command kept him away from Mount Vernon for more than eight years.

His military experiences, while more extensive than those of most other available candidates, hardly prepared him for the rigors of this command. Washington led what began as an untrained volunteer army of farmers and shopkeepers against what was then the world's largest and best-equipped fighting force. After numerous setbacks and defeats, Washington's steadfast determination, bold leadership, and often daring maneuvers began working in his army's favor. His courageous surprise attack on the Hessians at Trenton on December 26, 1776, is often seen as a turning point of the war. With vital financial and military support from France, victory was finally achieved at Yorktown in October 1781. Hostilities between Great Britain and the fledgling United States of America formally ended with the Treaty of Paris, signed two years later.

On December 23, 1783, Washington presented himself before Congress in Annapolis, Maryland, and resigned his command. Like Cincinnatus, a leader of the ancient Roman Republic whose conduct he greatly admired, Washington wisely relinquished power rather than lead the young nation as its king. He left Annapolis for Mount Vernon, determined never again to serve in public life. Despite his resolve, and his desire for a peaceful life on his beloved plantation, in the spring of 1787 he ended this self-imposed retirement to preside over the Constitutional Convention in Philadelphia. When the first presidential election was held, two years later, he received the vote of every elector—a victory that makes him the only unanimously elected president in U.S. history.

During the first of Washington's two terms as president (1789–93), he was primarily occupied with organizing the executive branch of the new government and establishing effective and efficient administrative procedures. A keen judge of character and talent, he surrounded himself with the ablest men in the new nation. He appointed his former aide-de-camp Alexander Hamilton as secretary of the treasury, his former artillery chief, Henry Knox, as secretary of war, and Thomas Jefferson as secretary of state. James Madison was one of his principal advisors. In touring the northern and southern states, Washington learned that the American people were generally supportive of the new federal government. He planned, therefore, to step down at the end of his four-year term. But his cabinet members convinced him that only he could command the respect of members of both burgeoning political parties. Jefferson visited Washington at Mount Vernon to urge him to accept a second term, and though he longed to return home permanently, the president reluctantly agreed.

Foreign affairs dominated Washington's second term (1793–97), which was marred by a deepening partisanship in his administration. The French Revolution, which had erupted in 1789, and the outbreak of a general European war four years later forced him to make a crucial decision about America's role in European affairs. War, he concluded, would be disastrous for commerce and shatter the new nation's finances. Avoiding war would give the United States a chance to grow stronger. Thus Washington established the principle of neutrality in overseas conflicts that would shape American foreign policy for more than a century.

In 1797 Washington was finally able to retire and devote his last years to Mount Vernon. Sadly, his retirement was short-lived. On December 12, 1799, he was caught in sleet and snow while out riding and contracted a throat infection that soon cut off his breathing. Characteristically, he faced death with courage, saying, "I die hard, but I am not afraid to go." With his wife at his side, Washington died at about 10 p.m. on December 14. As news of his passing spread, the nation mourned.

General Henry (Light-Horse Harry) Lee, a Revolutionary War comrade, famously eulogized Washington:

First in war, first in peace, and first in the hearts of his countrymen, he was second to none in humble and enduring scenes of private life. Pious, just, humane, temperate, and sincere—uniform, dignified, and commanding—his example was as edifying to all around him as were the effects of that example lasting. . . . Correct throughout, vice shuddered in his presence and virtue always felt his fostering hand.

More than 200 years after Washington's death, the lasting example Lee extolled remains strong. His legacies were numerous and varied—in architecture, farming, business, and education. As both soldier and statesman, George Washington helped shape the world he left behind.

TO LEARN MORE

Excellent books include: *Washington: A Life* (2010) by Ron Chernow; *His Excellency: George Washington* (2004) by Joseph J. Ellis; *Realistic Visionary: A Portrait of George Washington* (2006) by Peter R. Henriques; and *1776* (2005) by David McCullough. Plentiful biographical information can also be found on our website, MountVernon.org.

RIGHT: *A brass-studded leather trunk that Washington used during the Revolutionary War.*
OPPOSITE: *Gilbert Stuart's iconic portrait of Washington, painted about 1804.*

George Washington was greeted with much fanfare on arriving in New York harbor in April 1789 for his inauguration as the first U.S. president. John C. McRae depicted the event in this 1867 engraving. RIGHT: *The inauguration prompted production of assorted commemorative and patriotic clothing buttons.*

LONG

FOURTH 1789 MEMORABLE
MARCH THE

This pastel likeness of Martha Washington is based on Gilbert Stuart's unfinished 1796 portrait. OPPOSITE: *One of her intricately carved and painted Chinese fans.*

MEET *Martha Washington*

TOP TO BOTTOM: *A miniature portrait of Martha Washington by James Peale (1796); her sewing workbasket; her gold-and-agate snuff-box; and the richly decorated slippers she wore to her wedding in 1759.*

Martha Dandridge, a daughter of Virginia's Tidewater gentry, was well positioned to become a plantation mistress. She played that part with consummate skill, first in marriage to one of Virginia's wealthiest men, Daniel Parke Custis, and then as George Washington's trusted partner. Ultimately, of course, she assumed other, more public roles—as a general's wife, as a president's wife, and finally as an inspiring symbol for the new nation. She adapted to these responsibilities with resolve and grace.

The relationship between George and Martha sustained them through personal tragedy as well as the difficult years of war and the presidency. Although Martha adored her husband, she was not overly deferential to him. It is said that when Martha, more than a foot shorter than George, wanted to get his attention, she pulled on his shirt collar to bring his face down to her level.

She was born on June 2, 1731, into a family of respectable planters who owned a comfortable home on a 500-acre plantation, about 35 miles from the colonial capital at Williamsburg. When Martha came of age, she was courted by Daniel Parke Custis. He owned thousands of acres of land and nearly 300 slaves and sat on the Governor's Council, the six-member upper chamber of the colony's general assembly. Married in 1750, the couple moved into Daniel's home, called White House.

There, Martha gave birth to four children, two of whom survived: John (Jacky) Parke Custis, born in 1754, and Martha (Patsy) Parke Custis, born in 1756. In 1757 Daniel Custis became gravely ill. Although Martha summoned the best physicians available, her husband soon died. She was a 26-year-old widow with two small children.

Less than a year later, in March 1758, she met George Washington. Their attraction was immediate, mutual, and powerful. Martha was charming, attractive, and of course wealthy. George, who was about six feet two inches tall (compared to Martha, who stood slightly over five feet), was an imposing figure whose reputation as a military leader preceded him.

Within months of meeting, they began planning a future together. Washington had already begun an expansion of Mount Vernon's Mansion, and Martha ordered her wedding finery from London. On January 6, 1759, they married at her home in New Kent County.

In the years before the Revolutionary War, the couple lived as genteel Virginia plantation owners. Martha's life revolved around her two surviving young children, Jacky and Patsy. Although Martha was in her late twenties when she and George were wed, the couple did not have children of their own—likely a disappointment to them both. Tragedy struck when Patsy died, probably of epilepsy, in 1773, and again eight years later, when Jacky succumbed to "camp fever" (typhus) at age 26, soon after joining General Washington at Yorktown as a civilian aide. When Jacky's widow, Eleanor, remarried, in 1783, the youngest two of her four children—Eleanor (Nelly) Parke Custis, then four years old, and George Washington (Washy) Parke Custis, then two years old—remained at Mount Vernon, where their paternal grandmother, Martha, and George Washington reared them as their own.

Martha's life was permanently altered by her husband's military career. During each of the eight years of war, she undertook the hard journey to wherever the Continental Army was making winter camp. (Ultimately, she would spend about half the war with her husband.) Martha was the general's sounding board and closest confidante. She acted as his secretary (copying letters) and represented him at official functions.

OPPOSITE: *This stylish, brown-silk 1790s gown was a favorite of Mrs. Washington.* BELOW: *Her music book, which George Washington inscribed with her name shortly after their wedding.*

She comforted sick and wounded soldiers and organized social activities to help boost camp morale.

Once Washington was elected president under the new U.S. Constitution, his wife faced additional challenges. In mid-May 1789, several weeks after the inauguration, Martha, the two grandchildren, and seven house slaves set off for New York City, the temporary national capital. (Philadelphia became the capital less than two years later.) In her new role, she was responsible not only for managing the presidential household but also for supervising domestic affairs at Mount Vernon from a distance. Just as her husband realized that his every action might set a precedent for future presidents, so Martha knew that her demeanor and actions would have consequences for the wives of future chief executives.

On Friday evenings, she hosted informal receptions at the presidential residence for members of Congress, visiting dignitaries, and local residents with proper social credentials. After being presented to her, guests enjoyed refreshments and conversation. They addressed their hostess as "our Lady Presidentess" and "Lady Washington." In time, Martha won over skeptics who complained that these weekly gatherings evoked a monarchy. On the contrary, opening up the president's house was a sign that the government would be receptive to the people.

In March 1797, Martha Washington returned to her beloved home at Mount Vernon. Now 65 years old, she suffered from various ailments and the infirmities of age but nonetheless embraced the challenges of resuming a normal family life. In addition, she made sure that the nearly constant stream of guests were graciously accommodated, fed, and, often, entertained.

Martha's grandchildren continued to be a source of joy. Although the oldest two did not live with the Washingtons, she was very fond of them both. Her particular favorite was Nelly, who married George's nephew Lawrence Lewis in the Mansion in February 1799.

When George Washington died, on December 14, 1799, so did Martha's hopes of spending many years with him at Mount Vernon. In the months that followed, she received countless condolence letters and hundreds of requests for mementos. She handled the onslaught of visitors and correspondence as best she could. But, fatigued and grieving, she often delegated routine household tasks and secretarial duties to trusted aides, servants, and family members.

In his will, Washington had provided that the 123 slaves he held outright (separate from the dower slaves, who would be distributed among the Custis heirs) were to gain their freedom after his wife's death. At the urging of her husband's nephew Bushrod Washington, Martha, who feared the slaves might hasten her death in order to gain their freedom, emancipated George Washington's slaves on January 1, 1801.

Martha's health declined precipitously, and she died on May 22, 1802. She was widely admired and beloved, and a posthumous tribute printed in an Alexandria, Virginia, newspaper aptly called her "the worthy partner of the worthiest of men."

TO LEARN MORE

Valuable sources include: *Martha Washington: An American Life* (2005) by Patricia Brady; *Martha Washington: First Lady of Liberty* (2002) by Helen Bryan; *Martha Washington: A Brief Biography* (2002) by Ellen McCallister Clark; and *Founding Mothers: The Women Who Raised Our Nation* (2004) by Cokie Roberts. Biographical information can also be found on our website, MountVernon.org.

TOP TO BOTTOM: *A miniature portrait of Martha Washington from about 1790, attributed to John Ramage; one of 12 cross-stitched, seashell-pattern chair cushions she crafted between 1765 and sometime after 1794; one of her sequined white-silk slippers; and an English porcelain songbird that once graced the Washingtons' dinner table.*

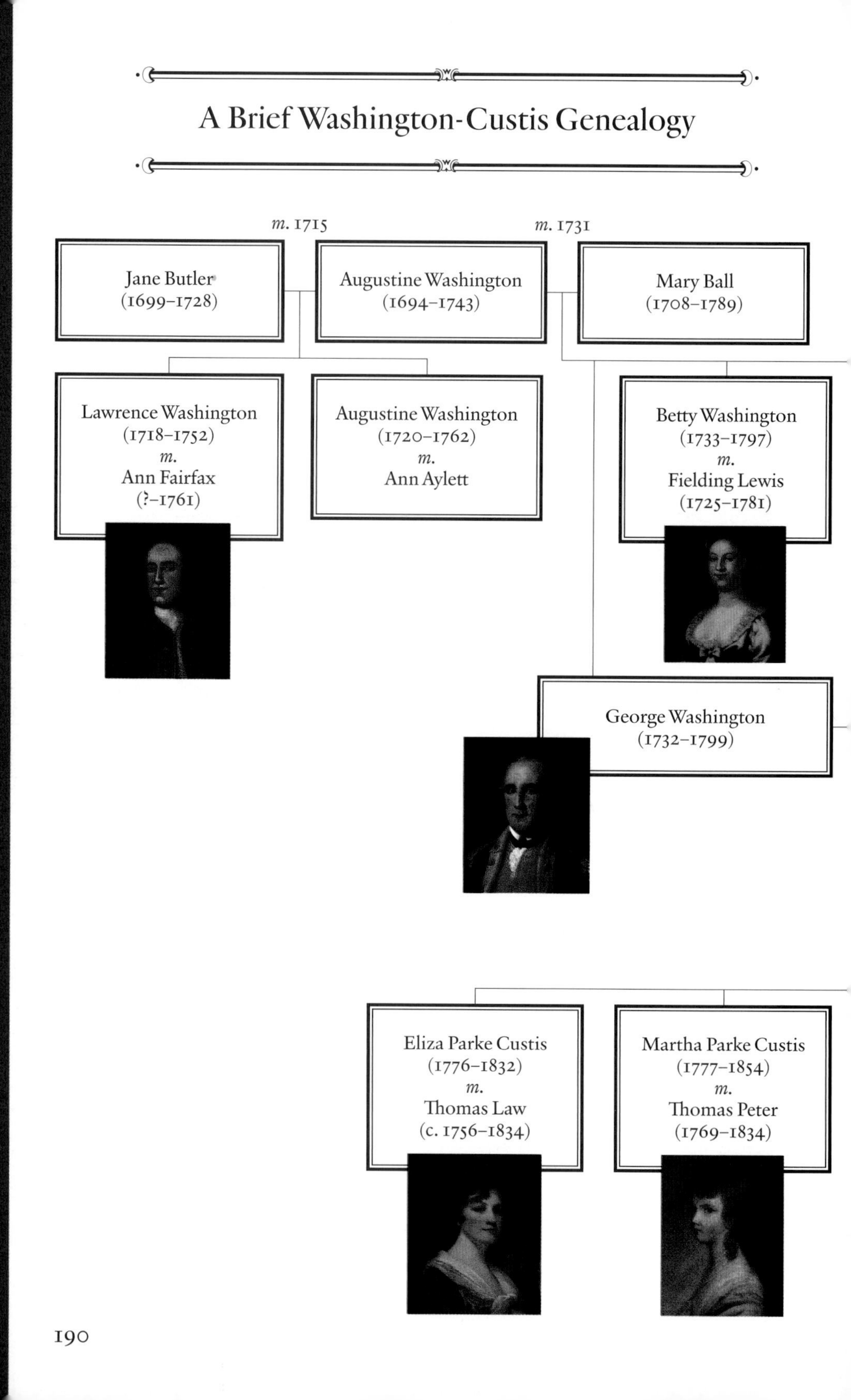

A Brief Washington-Custis Genealogy
m. 1715
m. 1731
Jane Butler (1699–1728)
Augustine Washington (1694–1743)
Mary Ball (1708–1789)
Lawrence Washington (1718–1752) m. Ann Fairfax (?–1761)
Augustine Washington (1720–1762) m. Ann Aylett
Betty Washington (1733–1797) m. Fielding Lewis (1725–1781)
George Washington (1732–1799)
Eliza Parke Custis (1776–1832) m. Thomas Law (c. 1756–1834)
Martha Parke Custis (1777–1854) m. Thomas Peter (1769–1834)

"I must request you will accept my acknowledgments . . . for the trouble you have taken in making genealogical collections relative to the family of Washington."

—George Washington to Sir Isaac Heard, Philadelphia, May 2, 1792

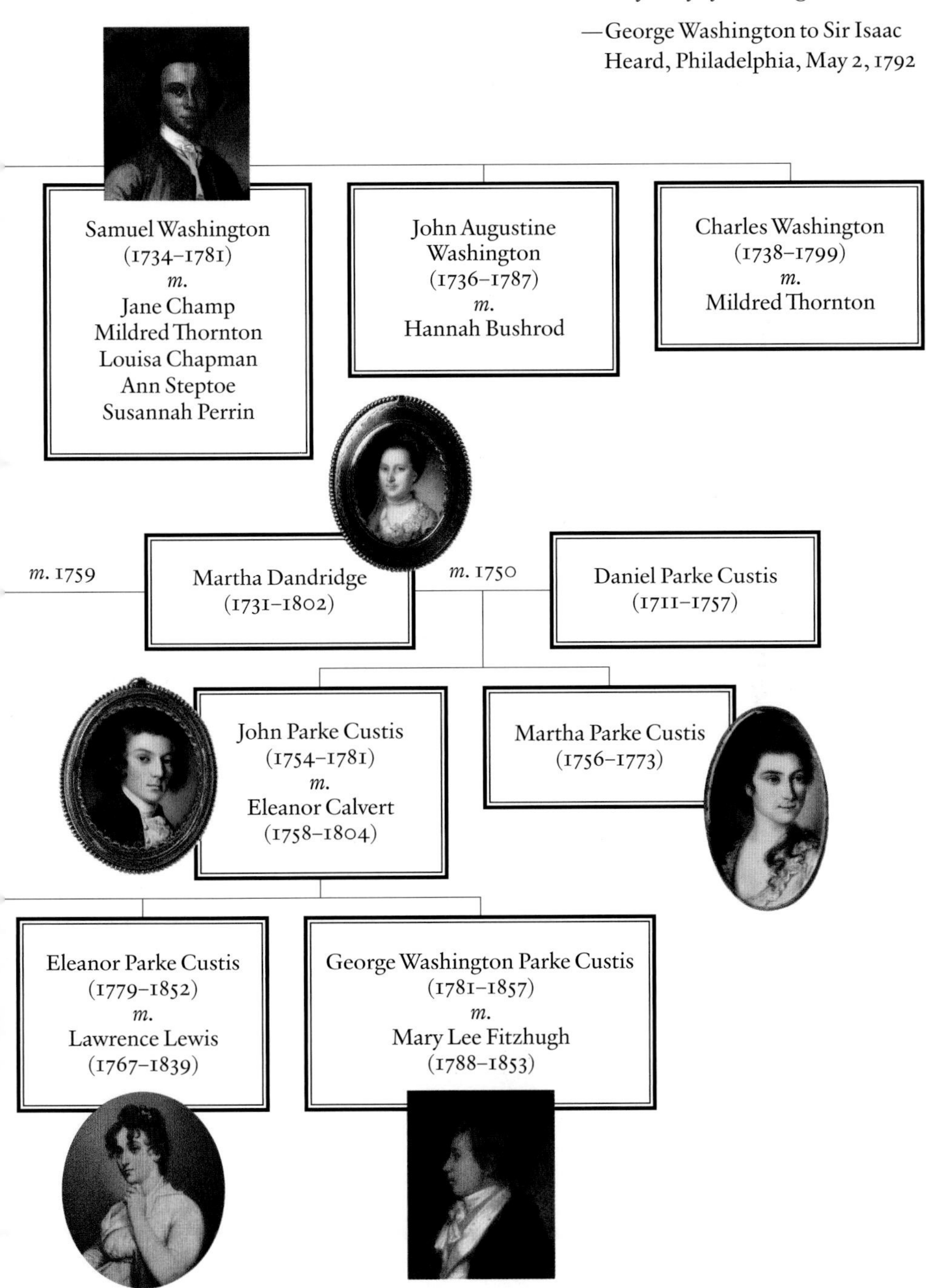

BELOW: *The hearth area in the women's bunk room of the greenhouse slave quarters.* OPPOSITE: *A clay pipe excavated at Mount Vernon. Typical of ones used in the 1750s and 1760s, this pipe may have belonged to a Washington slave.*

Slavery at Mount Vernon

George Washington's life on his "pleasantly situated" estate relied almost entirely on slave labor. Slaves worked the fields that were a key basis of his wealth. They also built the Mansion and its many outbuildings, erected the walls on the grounds, dug the orchard and gardens, polished the fine furniture and silver, slaughtered hogs for the hams in which Martha Washington took pride, ground wheat at the gristmill, and stirred mash at the distillery. They cooked and served meals, washed dishes, made butter and cheese, chopped wood for and tended fires in the fireplaces, fed and groomed horses, made clothes, hauled water for bathing, and cared for small children.

Of those individuals living at Mount Vernon in 1799, the year Washington died, the vast majority were slaves—316 of the total population of about 340. George Washington owned some of them, while others, called "dower slaves," belonged to the estate of Martha Washington's first husband, Daniel Parke Custis.

Extensive research in recent decades has clarified the facts of slave life on the estate. Although Washington was considered an enlightened slaveholder who granted his slaves certain limited freedoms, they nevertheless labored for the benefit of others, lived in poverty, and were victims of a system that viewed them as property. Tobias Lear, the general's personal secretary and friend, lived at Mount Vernon for a time and noted in March 1789 that Washington's "negroes are not treated as blacks in general are in this Country, they are clothed and fed as well as any labouring people whatever and they are not subject to the lash or a domineering Overseer but still they are slaves."

The majority of Mount Vernon's slaves were agricultural workers, most of whom lived on the estate's four outlying farms. Women, who were on the lowest rung of the plantation-economy ladder, generally were field hands. Slaves were expected to work from sunup to sundown, with Sundays off. Some also were granted three or four days off at Christmas as well as the Mondays after Easter and Pentecost.

George Washington was born into a world that accepted slavery as a form of labor and became a slaveholder himself at

age 11, when he inherited 10 slaves through his father's will. No doubt, his attitude toward slavery before the Revolutionary War was typical of other wealthy Virginia planters. Many historians, however, believe that his experiences during the war altered his viewpoint. By the 1780s, he had forbidden his overseers from using the whip without first conducting an investigation of the alleged wrongdoing. He wrote that discipline was better accomplished by watchfulness and warnings than by severity. He also decided, according to an August 1799 letter, not to buy or sell any more slaves, writing, "To disperse the families I have an aversion."

By limiting harsher forms of punishment, Washington lessened a plantation owner's most powerful means of coercion. At the same time, however, he wanted the slaves to work even harder. He had come home from the war determined to make Mount Vernon a model of agriculture for the new nation—a goal that required plenty of manual labor. To motivate the slaves, Washington offered rewards for work well done, including, occasionally, money and chances to advance; a few of his slaves even became overseers themselves. Perhaps not surprisingly, some slaves on the estate did not embrace their master's vision and chafed under the system.

Washington often stated after the war that he would support legislative efforts to abolish slavery, but he could not bring himself to lead that movement. Perhaps he feared that if he publicly took that stand, the southern states would secede—as they ultimately did seven decades later, sparking the Civil War. He had worked too hard to help form the country to risk it being torn apart.

By the end of the Revolutionary War, Washington was talking about freeing his slaves and hoped Virginia would enact a statewide plan for gradual emancipation. That hope proved to be futile, and by the early 1790s he was privately taking steps to free both his own and the Custis dower slaves. In the end, however, he was able to emancipate only those individuals who were his property outright—a little less than half of the enslaved population at Mount Vernon.

TO LEARN MORE

- For a book of essays on this complex subject, see *Slavery at the Home of George Washington* (2001), edited by Philip J. Schwarz.
- In observance of Black History Month every February, Mount Vernon offers programs highlighting the lives and contributions of the slaves who lived and worked here. Each day in February, a wreath-laying ceremony takes place at the Slave Memorial (see page 135).
- The everyday lives and contributions of slaves on the estate are the focus of various programs year-round. For details, inquire at the Ford Orientation Center information desk.
- Information about slavery at Mount Vernon can also be found on our website, MountVernon.org

OPPOSITE: *Eastman Johnson's 1857 painting* The Old Mount Vernon *provides a rare glimpse of enslaved life at the estate in the mid-19th century.*

FROM GEORGE WASHINGTON'S LAST WILL AND TESTAMENT

"It is my Will & desire that all the Slaves which I hold in my *own right*, shall receive their freedom. . . . And whereas among those who will recieve freedom according to this devise, there may be some, who from old age or bodily infirmities, and others who on account of their infancy, that will be unable to support themselves; it is my Will and desire that all who come under the first & second description shall be comfortably cloathed & fed by my heirs while they live; and that such of the latter description as have no parents living, or if living are unable, or unwilling to provide for them, shall be bound by the Court until they shall arrive at the age of twenty five years; and in cases where no record can be produced, whereby their ages can be ascertained, the judgment of the Court, upon its own view of the subject, shall be adequate and final. The Negros thus bound, are (by their Masters or Mistresses) to be taught to read & write; and to be brought up to some useful occupation, agreeably to the Laws of the Commonwealth of Virginia, providing for the support of Orphan and other poor Children."

ABOVE: *This is one of several bells in the original bell system that was used to summon slaves and servants to specific locations within the Mansion.* BELOW: *One of the few surviving handmade bowls that Mount Vernon's enslaved cooks used to prepare food for the Washingtons and their many visitors.* OPPOSITE: *Washington drew up this list of slaves at the estate in July 1790.*

Negros

Belonging to George Washington in his own right and by Marriage

G.W

Tradesmen &c.

Names	ages	Remarks
Nat . Smith		His wife Lucy D.R. dow
George . Do		Ditto Lydia R.T. Do
Isaac . Carpr		... Kitty Dairy Do
James . Do	40	... Darcus M.H. G.W
Sambo . Do		... Agnes R.T. dow
Davy . Do		... Edy U.T. G.W
Joe . Do		... Dolshy Spinr dow
Tom . Coopr		... Nanny M.H. G.W
Moses . Do		No Wife
Jacob . Do		Ditto
George . Gardr		His wife Sall D.R. dow
Harry . Do		No wife
Boatswain Ditchr		His wife Myrtilla Spinr G.W
Dundee . Do		His wife at Mr Lears
Charles . Do		Ditto Fanny U.F. dowr
Ben . Do		Ditto Penny R.T. G.W
Ben . Miller		Ditto Sinah Mn H dow
Forester Do		No Wife
Nathan Cook	31	Wife Peg M.H. G.W
Muclus B.Layr		Do Capt Marshalls
Cuba . Carter		No wife
Matilda Spinner		Boson Ditcher
Frank H. Servt		Wife Lucy Cook
Will . Shoemr		Lame no wife
Amount	24	

Dower

Tradesmen &c.

Names	ages	Remarks
Tom Davis B.Layr		wife at Mr Lears
Simms . Carp		Do Daphne Frenchs
Cyrus . Postn		Do Lucy R.T. G.W
Wilson . Ditto	15	no wife
Godfrey Cartr		Wife Mima Mn Ho dowr
James . Do		Do Alla Do Do
Hanson . Distr		No wife
Peter . Do		Ditto
Nat . Do		Ditto
Daniel . Do		Ditto
Timothy . Do		
Ha: Joe . Ditchr		Wife Sylla D.R. G.W
Christ . H. Servt		Do Majr Washns
Marcus . Do		No Wife
Lucy . Cook		Husbd H. Frank G.W
Matey Charlotte Sempss		No Husband No husband
Sall . H. Md		Do
Caroline Do		Husbd Peter Hardman
Kitty . Milkd		Do Isaac Carpr G.W
Alce . Spinr		Charles Freeman
Betty Davis Do		Mrs Washingtons Dick
Dolshy		Husbd Joe Carpr G.W
Anna		Do lives at George Town
Judy	21	No Husband
Delphy		Ditto Do
Peter Lame Knitter		No wife
Alla . Do		Husbd James Cart dow
Amount	28	

Mansion House (G.W)

Passed Labour

Names	ages	Remarks
Frank	80	No Wife
Gunner	90	Wife Judy R.T. G.W
Sam Cook	40	Ditto Alce M.H. Do

Mansion House (Dower)

Names	ages	Remarks
Will		Wife Aggy D.R. G.W
Joe . Postilr		Do Sall R.T. Do
Mike		No Wife son to Lucy
Sinah		Husbd Miller Ben G.W
Mima		Do Godfrey Wagr dowr
Lucy		No Husband
Grace		Husbd Mr Lears Juba
Letty		No husband
Nancy		Ditto Do
Viner		Ditto Do
Eve	17	Ditto a dwarf
Delia	14	Ditto her sister

Children

Names	ages	Remarks
Phil		son to Lucy
Patty		daughter to Do

BELOW: *An 1858 photograph of the Mansion's east front, showing the piazza nearing collapse—supported by old ship masts.* OPPOSITE: *The badge of the Mount Vernon Ladies' Association, worn by members when they are on the estate.*

The Rescue and Restoration of Mount Vernon

On a moonlit night in the fall of 1853, the captain of a steamship cruising down the Potomac River past Mount Vernon ordered the customary tribute to George Washington's home: the tolling of a bell. As passenger Louisa Cunningham strolled out on deck, she was shocked to see what time and the elements had done to the Mansion. As Mrs. Cunningham, a native Virginian, wrote to her daughter in South Carolina:

> *I was painfully distressed at the ruin and desolation of the home of Washington, and the thought passed through my mind: Why was it the women of his country did not try to keep it in repair, if the men could not do it?*

Ann Pamela Cunningham took up her mother's challenge, launching an ambitious effort to rescue and restore Mount Vernon. The organization she established, the Mount Vernon Ladies' Association of the Union, continues to safeguard the Washington legacy and oversee operation of the estate to this day.

Ann Pamela Cunningham (1816–1875), founder and first Regent of the Mount Vernon Ladies' Association.

Miss Cunningham began her monumental task by sending a letter to the *Charleston Mercury* that the paper published on December 2, 1853. In an era when it was thought fitting for a lady's name to appear in a newspaper only when she married or died, her plea to the "Ladies of the South" to save Mount Vernon was signed "A Southern Matron." When the appeal resulted in the formation of small societies and donations from throughout the South, she expanded her outreach to include the northern states. From then on, she boldly signed her name to published letters.

The first meeting of the Mount Vernon Ladies' Association was held in 1854. Miss Cunningham served as Regent, presiding over a group of Vice Regents, each representing a different state; more than 150 years later, the Association maintains the same organizational structure. In 1860 its members finalized their purchase of the Mansion and 200 acres of adjoining land from the first president's great-great nephew John Augustine Washington III, who could not afford to maintain the estate. The Association promptly got to work shoring up the dilapidated buildings and opened the American landmark to the public that same year.

Restoration halted during the Civil War. Union and Confederate soldiers alike visited to honor George Washington's memory, most of whom respectfully laid down their arms before entering the property. When the war ended, the Association set about furnishing the house artfully, combining a handful of Washington-owned pieces with an assortment of 18th-century objects and more recent items. As the collection grew and standards for historic preservation rose, the Association became able to furnish the house with many of the Washingtons' personal items and others that reflected their tastes and social standing.

Among several crucial decisions the Association faced was whether to install electricity in the house, which it did in 1916 under the personal supervision of Thomas Edison—acknowledging that electric lights would be safer than kerosene lamps and candles.

Determined to preserve Mount Vernon as it appeared in 1799, the year Washington died, the Association in the 1930s removed a porch from the Mansion and the balustrade atop its piazza—both built by the president's nephew Bushrod Washington in the early 1800s. In 1951 the Association reconstructed Washington's greenhouse and slave quarters, which had burned down in 1835. Scholarly research conducted on the Mansion in the 1970s prompted experts to analyze microscopically the original paint colors of the home's interior. And in 1987, an archaeology department was established to study sites around the estate in order to provide new insights into the daily activities of Mount Vernon's original residents.

With the rapid population expansion of the Washington, D.C., area after World War II, new real estate developments began threatening one of Mount Vernon's most beloved features: the remarkable view George Washington enjoyed across the Potomac. In 1955 an oil-tank facility and sewage-treatment plant were proposed for 500 acres right across the river. Led by Frances Payne Bolton, who was Vice Regent for Ohio as well as a U.S. Congresswoman, the Association enlisted support from the National Park Service, Maryland neighbors, and environmentalists nationwide to preserve the opposite shoreline for future generations. Efforts to protect the view—which spans 80 square miles—continue today.

The Association continues to encourage public understanding of Washington, exploring his roles as a farmer, businessman, slaveholder, and Father of Our Country. In recent decades, the organization has overseen the addition to Mount Vernon of the Pioneer Farm and also re-created Washington's gristmill and distillery. In 2006 the Donald W. Reynolds Museum and Education Center and the Ford Orientation Center opened, offering exhibits focused on Washington's early years, his military and political careers, and his legacy. In 2013 the Fred W. Smith National Library for the Study of George Washington—the long-overdue equivalent of a presidential library for the nation's first chief executive—opened.

As America's oldest historic-preservation organization, the Association has often served as a model for historic sites nationwide. Relying on admissions, retail and concession sales, and private donations, the Association supports Mount Vernon without accepting grants from the federal government or from state and local governments, and no tax dollars are spent to help carry out its mission.

The Mount Vernon Ladies' Association continues to honor and live by the parting challenge Miss Cunningham posed in a letter written when she retired as Regent, in 1874:

> *Ladies, the Home of Washington is in your charge. See to it that you keep it the Home of Washington! Let no irreverent hand change it; no vandal hands desecrate it with the fingers of—progress! Those who go to the Home in which he lived and died, wish to see in what he lived and died! Let one spot in this grand country of ours be saved from 'change!' Upon you rests this duty.*

Miss Cunningham (seated, looking at Houdon's bust of Washington) with 11 early Vice Regents of the Mount Vernon Ladies' Association in 1873.

Dusk begins settling over the Mansion's east lawn, the Potomac, and the Maryland shore on a fall evening.

ILLUSTRATION CREDITS

Gavin Ashworth: 3, 11, 43, 44–45, 46, 47, 48 (bottom), 49, 116, 141 (left), 149 (lower left), 170 (riding crop and spyglass), 172, 173, 174 (bottom), 178, 184 (bottom), back cover
Steven T. Bashore: 16 (right), 104 (bottom), 167
Eric Benson: 18–19
Ron Blunt: 106 (bottom), 107, 108, 109, 110–11, 192
Lee Boynton: 160 (bottom)
Will Brown: 70 (bottom)
Scot Bryant: 102
Renée Comet Photography: cover, 32, 62, 88–89, 93 (bottom), 120, 121 (all), 122–23, 126 (left), 128 (both), 138 (bottom)
Harry Connolly: 1, 77 (both), 85, 92, 117, 149 (top, center, and bottom right), 157 (center), 190 (L. Washington)
Hal Conroy: 75, 139 (top), 140 (top), 155 (top)
Conservation Center for Art and Historic Artifacts, Philadelphia: 141 (right), 197
Robert Creamer: 12 (left), 16 (left), 26, 30, 144 (both), 152–53, 155 (bottom), 157 (top), 158 (all), 159, 166
Samantha Dorsey: 183
Mark Finkenstaedt: 7, 21, 38 (top left), 63 (ceiling detail), 78 (top and bottom left), 81 (lower left, top left, and top right), 87 (right), 125 (right), 145, 154 (bottom), 161, 165, 168, 169, 170 (watch), 175 (bottom), 180 (bottom), 181 (bottom, all), 184 (workbasket), 186, 190 (E. P. Custis Law), 191 (J. P. Custis and M. P. Custis), 194
Russell Flint: 6, 14 (left), 17, 57, 58, 59 (top), 61, 98–99, 105, 132, 137, 156, 157 (bottom), 160 (top), 163
Greystone Pictures: 28–29
Mark Gulezian: 148
P. R. Gulley Studio: 154 (top)
John Henley: front endpaper, 13 (right), 24, 36–37, 40 (bottom), 112 (both), 124, 129 (top), 142–43, 204–5, back cover
Historic Kenmore: 190 (B. W. Lewis)
W. G. Hook, Architectural Illustration: back endpaper (map)
Amanda Isaac: 25, 95
Paul Kennedy: 50, 106 (top), 184 (top), 191 (E. P. Custis Lewis)
Anne Kingery: 87 (left), 196 (top)
Robert C. Lautman: 64–65, 67, 68, 72, 76, 79, 83, 86, 90, 97, 100 (all), 134 (top), 189 (slipper), 191 (S. Washington)
Peter Leach: 69
Taylor Lewis: 133
Todd Lindeman: 27, 39 (all), 146–47
Howard Marler: 22
Calvin McWhirter: 42, 104 (top), 118 (top left), 139 (bottom), 164 (bottom)
Mount Vernon Ladies' Association: 15 (right), 34–35 (bottom), 55 (all), 56 (both), 59 (bottom), 70 (top), 71 (top), 80, 91, 94 (top), 96, 101, 103 (all), 119, 135, 138 (top), 140 (bottom), 170 (top), 174–75 (top), 176, 179, 180–81 (top), 190 (G. Washington), 191, (M. Dandridge), 193, 198, 199, 202–3
J. Dean Norton: 13 (left), 15 (left), 118 (lower left), 129 (bottom)
Kevin O'Rourke: 164 (top)
Edward Owen: 48 (top), 81 (lower right), 184 (snuffbox), 187, 189 (top and bottom), 196 (bottom)
Dennis J. Pogue: front flap, 41, 94 (bottom)
Lisa Pregent: 118 (top right and bottom right)
Karen Price: 18–19
Katherine Ridgway: 182
Robert Shenk: 136
Walter Smalling, Jr.: 10, 12 (right), 51, 52–53, 54, 82, back flap
Studio TKM: 150 (top)
Ted Vaughan: 71 (bottom), 73 (both), 74, 78 (center), 150 (bottom), 190 (M. P. Custis Peter)
Virginia Tourism Corporation: 2, 40 (top), 115, 127
Jeff Watts: 189 (chair cushion)
Foster Wiley: 14 (right), 134 (bottom)
Sarah C. Wolfe: 8–9, 63 (bottom), 93 (top), 130–31

The Mount Vernon Ladies' Association is grateful to the following individuals and institutions for providing illustrations on the pages listed here:

Courtesy of an anonymous lender: 174 (bottom)
Courtesy of John T. Frey, Clerk, Fairfax Circuit Court, Quicksilver Photographers, LLC: 151
Courtesy of Division of Political History, National Museum of American History, Smithsonian Institution: 92
Courtesy, Collection of the State of South Carolina: 200
Courtesy of Peter Waddell: 34–35 (top)
Courtesy of the Washington-Custis-Lee Collection, Washington and Lee University, Lexington, Virginia: 66, 191 (G. W. P. Custis)

The efforts of the following staff members at George Washington's Mount Vernon were vital in creating this book:

Rebecca Aloisi, *Vice President for Marketing*
Dawn M. Bonner, *Manager of Visual Resources*
Jamie O. Bosket, *Vice President for Guest Experience*
Carol Borchert Cadou, *Senior Vice President for Historic Preservation and Collections*
Adam T. Erby, *Associate Curator*
Michael P. Kane, *Library Projects Assistant*
Stephen A. McLeod, *Director of Library Programs*
Julia Mosley, *Director of Retail*
J. Dean Norton, *Director of Horticulture*
James C. Rees, *former President and CEO (deceased)*
Susan P. Schoelwer, *Robert H. Smith Senior Curator*
Mary V. Thompson, *Research Historian*
Curtis G. Viebranz, *President and CEO*

Book design: Julia Sedykh Design
Initial text writer: Elizabeth MacBride
Managing editor: Stephen A. McLeod
Manuscript editor: Phil Freshman
Assistant manuscript editor (first edition): Susan C. Jones
Proofreaders: Phil Freshman and Stephen A. McLeod
Printing and binding: QuadGraphics, Taunton, MA
This book was typeset in MVB Verdigris and Galliard.

Third Edition, 2016

Published in the United States by the
Mount Vernon Ladies' Association
Post Office Box 110
Mount Vernon, VA 22121

Library of Congress Cataloging-in-Publication Data
George Washington's Mount Vernon estate, museum & gardens : official guidebook.
p. cm.
ISBN 978-0-931917-46-2 (pbk. : alk. paper) 1. Mount Vernon (Va. : Estate)—Guidebooks. 2. Washington, George, 1732–1799—Homes and haunts—Virginia—Mount Vernon (Estate) I. Mount Vernon Ladies' Association of the Union.
E312.5.G46 2012
975.5'291—dc23
2012024597

FACING TITLE PAGE: *A bird's-eye view of the Mansion, some of its surrounding outbuildings, and the Potomac River beyond.*

TITLE PAGE: *The original painted-metal dove of peace that crowned the weathervane atop the Mansion is on view in the Museum.*

Mount Vernon

- A Texas Gate (main entrance)
- B Lady Washington Shop, *p. 17*
- C Greenhouse Slave Quarters, *p. 109*
- D Greenhouse, *p. 128*
- E Interpretive Center
- F Blacksmith Shop, *p. 105*
- G Spinning Room and Overseer's Quarters, *p. 102*
- H Salt House, *p. 101*
- I Botanical Garden, *p. 128*
- J Gardener's House, *p. 101*
- K Servants' Hall, *p. 41*
- L Mansion Circle, *p. 114*
- M Kitchen, *p. 84*
- N Storehouse and Clerk's Quarters, *p. 91*